T Ewen Holmes
1994.

UNITING
in
WORSHIP

People's Book

Uniting Church Press
Melbourne

Published by
The Joint Board of Christian Education
Second Floor, 10 Queen Street, Melbourne 3000, Australia

Prepared by the Assembly Commission on Liturgy
and approved by the Assembly Standing Committee for use
in the Uniting Church in Australia.

First printed 1988

_____

Edited by Hugh McGinlay
Designed by Jennifer Richardson
Typeset by National Graphics
Printed by Singapore National Printers Ltd.

ISBN 0 85819 709 X

JB88/1317

Contents

                                                   Page

Preface   5

Baptism and Related Services
   Baptism and the Reaffirmation of Baptism
      called Confirmation   14
   Baptism of a Child   22
   A Congregational Reaffirmation of Baptism   29
   A Personal Reaffirmation of Baptism   37
   The Covenant Service   43

The Service of the Lord's Day
   Prayers Before the Service   56
   A Service of Word and Sacrament   58
   Communion Beyond the Gathered Congregation   72

Pastoral Services
   The Marriage Service   80
   Thanksgiving for the Gift of a Child   86
   A Service of Healing   90
   A Service of Reconciliation   96
   A Celebration of New Beginnings in Faith   99
   Reception of a Member by Transfer   102
   Reception of a Member-in-Association   105
   Commissioning of Elders   108

Resources for Worship

The Creeds of the Church   122
Statements of Faith   124
Canticles   135
Litanies   164
Vestry Prayers   206
A Treasury of Prayers   211
Selections from the Psalter   245

Acknowledgments   358

Preface

The Uniting Church in Australia was inaugurated on 22 June 1977. It was formed by the union of the Congregational, Methodist and Presbyterian Churches. At the inaugural Assembly, a Commission on Liturgy was appointed, with the responsibility of preparing orders of worship and other resources. The first Assembly also endorsed the continuing use of orders of service and worship books that were being used by the three denominations which came into union.

However, the new church was soon looking for worship resources that would reflect its new-found unity. *The Australian Hymn Book*, prepared by an ecumenical committee over a period of nine years, was published a few months after the Inauguration of the Uniting Church. Within a year or two of its publication, most Uniting congregations had purchased the new hymn book, and it became a sign of a new phase in christian worship and witness, as well as the expression of a desire to proclaim the christian faith in the Australian cultural context.

But a new church was also requiring new orders of service, so the initial work of the Commission on Liturgy was to prepare some basic orders – Baptism, Holy Communion, Ordination and Induction. These first services were published in a simple format, and congregations and presbyteries were given permission to reproduce them for their own needs.

Then, beginning in 1980 and concluding in 1985, twenty orders of service were published in a series of eight booklets, entitled *Uniting Church Worship Services*. Over the last few years, these booklets have been purchased in large numbers and have enjoyed wide use. The preparation of these provisional services gave the Commission opportunity to note new liturgical directions, ecumenically and internationally, as well as to reflect more deeply on the rich legacy of worship inherited from former denominational practice. These 'booklet' services also gave ministers, leaders of worship and congregations an opportunity to react to the new orders, and to send their comments and suggestions to the Commission.

It was at the Third Assembly in 1982 that a resolution directed the Commission 'to begin work on the publication of a comprehensive collection of services and other resources for use in worship'. *Uniting in Worship* is the result. After examination of the possibility of paperback collections, loose-leaf binders and similar options, the most practical format turned out to be a hardback service book.

Uniting in Worship is published in two editions: People's Book and Leader's Book. The latter contains many services not included in the People's Book; it also has the full text of each service. There are liturgical reasons as well as economic ones for having two books. The chief liturgical reason is that an outline of a service, with congregational responses in full, as in the People's Book, better enables the congregation to participate in the service than a complete text. The economic reasons have to do with the omission from the People's Book of those resources, such as the Lectionary, which do not need to be in the hands of the whole congregation.

Ministers and leaders of worship will need a copy of each edition, as the People's Book has selections from the Psalms and other resources which will be useful both for formal services and less formal ones. Some church members may also desire to have a copy of each edition, as the Leader's Book gives access to 'Resources for the Liturgical Year' and 'Resources for Leading Worship', but the intention is that the People's Book will be the one generally used in the congregation.

Although both books are in hardback, liturgical work, including revision of services, will continue. The publication of *Uniting in Worship* is not so much a point of arrival as a station on the way. The needs of the church are always in process of change, and the pace of change has been particularly rapid in recent decades. The provision of new services, and the revision of some of those in *Uniting in Worship*, will be needed during the 1990s. The question of when a hardback successor to *Uniting in Worship* will appear is unanswerable at this stage, but other denominations in the English-speaking world are mentioning twelve or fifteen years as the expected life of their service books or prayer books.

Since 1977, the Commission on Liturgy has been based in South Australia, but has had the benefit of consultants in all Australian states. Most of these are Uniting Church people, but valuable help has been received from members of other denominations and this help is gratefully acknowledged. We have also benefitted from published material and friendly advice from liturgical commissions in Canada, New Zealand, the United Kingdom and the United States.

As well as this lively correspondence, there have been drafting groups in several Australian cities, and these have lightened the load of the Commission considerably. Without their help, the publication date of 1988 would not have been possible. In the later stages of drafting, there have been two points of reference: the Assembly Commission on Doctrine (a national body); and the Assembly Standing Committee and its three working groups. These points of reference have enabled the Commission to propose confidently to the Assembly of 1988 that *Uniting in Worship* be authorised as 'official services of the Uniting Church in Australia'.

During the drafting process, many services have been field tested in congregations. The Commission is grateful for the co-operation of synods, presbyteries and parishes in the testing and evaluation of our work.

It can easily be seen that the process of producing *Uniting in Worship* has been an elaborate one. No book of services or prayers could claim to be without blemish, but the Commission is gratified by the keen participation of many individuals and groups within the Uniting Church and beyond. The Acknowledgments set out the published sources to which we are indebted but the individual ideas and suggestions used have been even greater in number.

The status and authority of published services is a matter of some debate within the Uniting Church. It is important to avoid both understatement and overstatement of the authority of *Uniting in Worship*. Its services and resources are not *required* to be used. Ministers and other worship leaders have the right to use other books, provided that these conform to the doctrine of the Uniting Church. On the other hand, *Uniting in Worship*, with the approval of the Assembly behind it, sets a standard for worship. It is normative in the sense that it is a standard against which other services may be measured.

This does not mean, of course, that the services in *Uniting in Worship* are intended to be used rigidly and without imagination. All worship should be geared to the particular situation of the congregation, be it large or small, urban or rural. All the resources in *Uniting in Worship* are therefore designed to be used in a flexible way. Indeed most of the services have many options within them, and there are frequent invitations to use free prayer. The Service of the Lord's Day, which is the centre-piece of the book, is a case in point. There is a variety of Great Prayers of Thanksgiving, and at other points in the service the entire content of a prayer must be provided by the leader and congregation. The funeral service contains the greatest number of options, as the Commission believes that many factors combine to make each funeral unique, one which requires careful choice between various possibilities.

But flexibility is more than choosing between printed options, or composing prayers of intercession, or other prayers for local use. Other factors such as the desired length of the service, the background and history of the congregation, and the people available for leadership will suggest variations from the printed text. This flexibility must be accompanied by responsibility, so that the congregation may be protected from worship which is idiosyncratic or insensitive.

The way in which these general principles apply to particular services and parts of services may be gleaned from *A Leader's Guide to Uniting in Worship* compiled by the Revd Robert Gribben. This volume is an important tool for all leaders of worship.

Uniting in Worship is not itself an authoritative statement of the church's doctine in the way that Assembly doctrinal pronouncements are. However the Commission has been guided by the doctrinal standards of our denomination. First among these are the Scriptures of the Old and New Testaments. The Commission has sought to use the Scripture in a way that reflects both the deep embedding of Scripture in the prayers of christian people and the development of biblical scholarship in recent decades. Second in importance comes the *Basis of Union* of the Uniting Church. Its statements on baptism and holy communion have been particularly important. Third comes the developing ecumenical consensus concerning worship and the sacraments. The crucial text here is *Baptism, Eucharist and Ministry* (World Council of Churches, 1982).

The commitment of the Uniting Church to christian unity has also meant that translations from ecumenical sources have been treated as having a strong claim for adoption in this book. The English Language Liturgical Consultation completed its work in time for its texts to be included in *Uniting in Worship* although the book of translations and commentary called *Praying Together* will not be published for some months. This international Consultation has an Australian counterpart, the Australian Consultation on Liturgy, and the discussions of that body, conducted annually since 1976, have been of great benefit to the Uniting Church.

The Commission has borrowed not only international translations but original prayers from other English-speaking churches. Some material is original to members of the Commission and other Uniting Church contributors. The style of language we have sought to adopt is contemporary but dignified, direct without being bland, and clear without being prosaic. It is not always understood that the language of worship (that is, for general use throughout the church, as distinct from the local and extempore) is not the same as everyday or conversational English. The words and many of the phrases will be common to both, but the tone and temper will be different. This means that the manner of reading is crucial. The more familiar the texts become, the greater is the possibility of good, prayerful reading.

The Commission has used inclusive language where the references are to human beings. The Assembly of the church has itself given a lead in this direction and the Commission has been glad to follow. We have not, however, extended this to include the names of God. While some female imagery is certainly appropriate with reference to God, biblical names which are male, especially Father and Son, are not to be discarded, as they belong to the heart of Trinitarian doctrine. More discussion of the use of inclusive language will take place in the church, and the Commission wishes to be part of that discussion.

Two of the services in this book are available in separate booklets, namely Baptism and Marriage. This provision is a response to pastoral experience with the use of the booklets in the *Uniting Church Worship Services* series.

It is expected that further resources, not included in *Uniting in Worship*, will follow in due time. Among these will be resources for daily prayer and Scripture reading.

There is little provision of music in *Uniting in Worship* because two other books provide this. *The Australian Hymn Book* (1977) is used widely. The supplementary book *Sing Alleluia* (1987) includes not only a good selection of contemporary christian songs but has several communion settings. These settings are recommended to ministers, musicians and congregations as a means to congregational participation in the prayers and proclamation of the eucharist.

Music and hymns, orders of service and resources for worship have power both to shape faith and to kindle devotion. But because they are human creations and words, they have their limitations. Aids to worship are signposts for christian pilgrims, not the goal of their journey. Only the grace of Jesus Christ and the power of the Holy Spirit can bring human words and works to life, enabling us to be true worshippers who worship the Father in spirit and in truth.

In offering *Uniting in Worship* to the church in the early part of our history as a denomination within the Church catholic, the Commission on Liturgy affirms Paragraph 18 of the *Basis of Union*:

> The Uniting Church affirms that she belongs to the people of God on the way to the promised end. She prays God that, through the gift of the Spirit, he will constantly correct that which is erroneous in her life, will bring her into deeper unity with other churches, and will use her worship, witness and service to his eternal glory through Jesus Christ the Lord.   Amen.

D'Arcy Wood
Chairperson
Assembly Commission on Liturgy

March, 1988

Members of the Assembly Commission on Liturgy, 1983-1988

Deaconess Pat Baker
Revd John Bentley
Revd David Brown
Ms Jessie Byrne-Hoffmann
Mr Graham Canty
Revd Grant Dunning
Secretary
Revd Robert Gribben
Mr Trevor Kitto

Revd Norah Norris
Miss Katherine O'Neill
Revd Dr Brian Phillips
Revd Michael Sawyer
Revd Graham Vawser
Revd John Watt
Revd Rob Williams
Revd Dr D'Arcy Wood
Chairperson

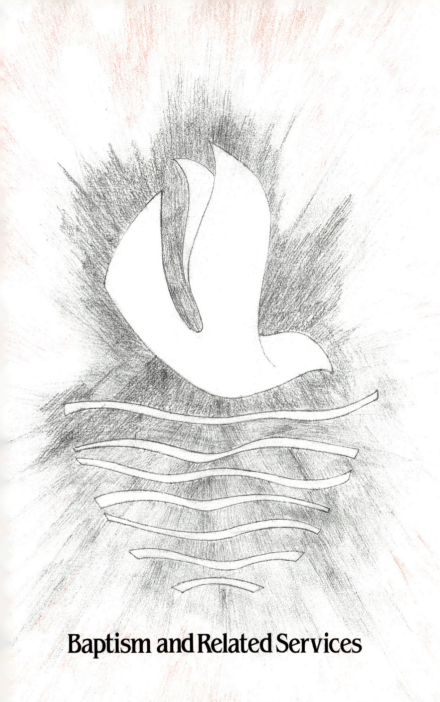

Baptism and Related Services

NOTES

i   This service is for the baptism and confirmation of people who profess faith in Jesus Christ and for the confirmation of such people who are already baptised.

ii This order forms part of the congregation's Sunday worship.

iii At the conclusion of each prayer, the people say or sing **Amen**.

Baptism
and the Reaffirmation of Baptism
Called Confirmation

1   HYMN

2   PRESENTATION

The candidates for baptism and/or confirmation are presented.

3   SCRIPTURE

4   THE MEANING OF BAPTISM AND
    CONFIRMATION

5   RENUNCIATION AND AFFIRMATION

The minister says to all the candidates:

Through baptism
we enter the convenant which God has established;
and in confirmation
we affirm that we belong to God's covenant people.

In the light of the gospel we proclaim,
I ask you now:

The minister addresses each candidate in turn:

N, do you repent of your sins?

I repent of my sins.

Do you turn to Jesus Christ,
who has defeated the power of sin and death
and brought us new life?

I turn to Christ.

Do you pledge yourself to God,
trusting in Jesus Christ as Saviour and Lord
and in the Holy Spirit as Counsellor and Guide?

I pledge myself to God.

The minister may touch each candidate's ears and mouth, saying:

N, may the Lord open your ears to receive his word,
and your mouth to proclaim his praise.

The minister says to the candidates and the congregation:

Let us confess the faith into which we are baptised.

The people stand.

Do you believe in God,
who made you and loves you?

I believe in God, the Father almighty,
creator of heaven and earth.

Do you believe in Jesus Christ,
your Saviour and Lord?

I believe in Jesus Christ, God's only Son, our Lord,
who was conceived by the Holy Spirit,
born of the Virgin Mary,
suffered under Pontius Pilate,
was crucified, died, and was buried;
he descended to the dead.
On the third day he rose again;
he ascended into heaven,
he is seated at the right hand of the Father,
and he will come to judge the living and the dead.

Do you believe in the Holy Spirit,
and the continuing work of our salvation?

I believe in the Holy Spirit,
the holy catholic Church,
the communion of saints,
the forgiveness of sins,
the resurrection of the body,
and the life everlasting. Amen.

> If there are candidates for baptism, those already baptised return
> to their places.
>
> If there are no baptisms, the service continues at 8, HYMN.
>
> The people remain standing.

6   PRAYER OF THANKSGIVING

> The elder pours water into the font.

The Lord be with you.
And also with you.

Lift up your hearts.
We lift them to the Lord.

Let us give thanks to the Lord our God.
It is right to give our thanks and praise.

> The minister offers a prayer of thanksgiving for the gift of water
> and its significance in salvation history and asks God's blessing on
> the water and the person(s) to be baptised.

7 THE BAPTISM

The people remain standing for the act of baptism.

NN, I baptise you
in the name of the Father,
and of the Son,
and of the Holy Spirit.

The people respond:

Amen.

The minister marks the sign of the cross on the forehead of the
newly-baptised person, and may say:

NN, from this day on
the sign of the cross is upon you.

The minister presents the baptised member to the congregation,
saying:

N is now received into the holy catholic Church
according to Christ's command.

8 HYMN

During the singing of the hymn, candidates for confirmation
come forward and stand with those newly baptised.

The people sit at the conclusion of the hymn.

9 LAYING ON OF HANDS

The minister says to the candidates:

Always remember you are baptised,
and be thankful.

Elders and other members appointed by the council of elders to lay on hands come forward and stand around the candidates.

Prayers are offered.

Hands are laid on the head of each candidate in turn and the minister says:

N, by the power of the Holy Spirit,
be a faithful witness to Christ
all the days of your life.

The candidates and the people respond each time this is said:
Amen.

The Aaronic Blessing may be said or sung by the people (*Australian Hymn Book*, 572), or said by the minister.

**The Lord bless you and keep you;
the Lord make his face to shine upon you,
and be gracious unto you;
the Lord lift up his countenance upon you,
and give you peace.**

Numbers 6:24-26

10 RESPONSES

One or more of the newly-confirmed members may make a brief statement of faith.

I ask you now to pledge yourself
to christian discipleship:

Do you promise to follow Christ
in your daily life?

**With God's help,
I will seek to love and obey Christ,
and to grow in my relationship with God
through prayer and study of the Bible.**

Do you promise to be a faithful member
of the christian community?

**With God's help,
I will share in the worship of the church,
and support its work
with my time, talents and money.**

Do you promise to participate
in God's mission to the world?

**With God's help,
I will witness to Christ in word and deed,
and look for the coming of his kingdom.**

The minister addresses the people:

I charge you,
the people of this congregation,
to love, encourage and support
these brothers and sisters in faith,
that they may continue to grow
in the grace of the Lord Jesus Christ
and the knowledge and love of God.

The people respond, saying:

**With God's help,
we will live out our baptism
as a loving community in Christ:
nurturing one another in faith,
upholding one another in prayer,
and encouraging one another in service.**

11 PRESENTATIONS

Gifts from the congregation, including the presentation of
baptism and/or confirmation certificates, may be made.

12 OFFERING

13 NOTICES AND CONCERNS OF THE CHURCH

14 PRAYERS OF THE PEOPLE

After each intercession, the following responses may be said or
sung:

Lord in your mercy,
hear our prayer.

or

Lord, hear us,
Lord, hear our prayer.

The Sacrament of the Lord's Supper

The service continues from page 64 in The Service of the Lord's
Day.

Baptismal candles may be presented after the final hymn.

NOTES

i   'The Uniting Church will baptise those who profess the christian faith, and children who are presented for baptism and for whose instruction and nourishment in the faith the church takes responsibility.' (*Basis of Union*, paragraph 7)

ii   This order forms part of the congregation's Sunday worship.

iii   At the conclusion of each prayer, the people say or sing **Amen**.

Baptism of a Child

1   HYMN

2   PRESENTATION

3   SCRIPTURE

4   THE MEANING OF BAPTISM

5   RENUNCIATION AND AFFIRMATION

The minister says to the parent(s):

N and N
what do you ask of God's church for N?

**We ask that he/she be baptised
into the faith and family of Jesus Christ.**

In the light of the covenant promise
and of your request,
I ask you now:

Do you believe that the gospel
enables us to turn from the darkness of evil
and to walk in the light of Christ?

We do.

N, may the Lord open your ears to receive his word,
and your mouth to proclaim his praise.

Let us confess the faith into which we are baptised.

The people stand.

Do you believe in God,
who made you and loves you?

**I believe in God, the Father almighty,
     creator of heaven and earth.**

Do you believe in Jesus Christ,
your Saviour and Lord?

**I believe in Jesus Christ, God's only Son, our Lord,
     who was conceived by the Holy Spirit,
     born of the Virgin Mary,
     suffered under Pontius Pilate,
     was crucified, died, and was buried;
     he descended to the dead.
     On the third day he rose again;
     he ascended into heaven,
     he is seated at the right hand of the Father,
     and he will come to judge the living and the dead.**

Do you believe in the Holy Spirit,
and the continuing work of our salvation?

I believe in the Holy Spirit,
the holy catholic Church,
the communion of saints,
the forgiveness of sins,
the resurrection of the body,
and the life everlasting. Amen.

The people remain standing.

6   PRAYER OF THANKSGIVING

The elder pours water into the font.

The Lord be with you.
And also with you.

Lift up your hearts.
We lift them to the Lord.

Let us give thanks to the Lord our God.
It is right to give our thanks and praise.

The minister offers a prayer of thanksgiving for the gift of water
and its significance in salvation history and asks God's blessing on
the water and the child to be baptised.

7   THE BAPTISM

The people remain standing for the act of baptism.

NN, I baptise you
in the name of the Father,
and of the Son,
and of the Holy Spirit.

The people respond:
Amen.

The minister marks the sign of the cross on the forehead of the child and may say:

NN, from this day on
the sign of the cross is upon you.

The minister presents the baptised member to the congregation, saying:

N is now received into the holy catholic Church
according to Christ's command.

The Aaronic Blessing may be said or sung by the people (Australian Hymn Book, 572) or said by the minister.

**The Lord bless you and keep you;
the Lord make his face to shine upon you,
and be gracious unto you;
the Lord lift up his countenance upon you,
and give you peace.**

Numbers 6:24-26

The people sit.

8   RESPONSES

The minister says to the parent(s):

N and N,
I ask you now to respond to God's graciousness to N
by making these solemn promises:

Will you provide for your child
a christian home of love and trust?

With God's help, we will.

Will you set before N
the example of a christian life,
and will you pray that he/she will learn the way of Christ?

With God's help, we will.

Will you encourage your child
to grow within the fellowship of the church,
so that he/she may come to faith in Christ?

With God's help, we will.

The minister addresses the people:

I charge you,
the people of this congregation,
to maintain the life of worship and service,
that this child and all the children among you
may grow in the grace of the Lord Jesus Christ
and the knowledge and love of God.

The people respond:

**With God's help,
we will live out our baptism
as a loving community in Christ:
nurturing one another in faith,
upholding one another in prayer,
and encouraging one another in service.**

9 PRAYERS

The following response may be used:

Lord, hear us.
Lord, hear our prayer.

10 PRESENTATION

A gift from the congregation, including the presentation of the
certificate of baptism, may be made.

11 HYMN

If a baptismal hymn or song was not sung at the beginning of the
service, it may be sung here.

The Service of the Lord's Day continues.

A baptismal candle may be presented after the final hymn.

A Congregational Reaffirmation of Baptism

NOTES

i   This service is intended for occasional use by the whole congregation. The Easter Vigil, Easter Day, or any other Sunday of the Easter season, including the Day of Pentecost, is an appropriate time for the whole congregation to join in a reaffirmation of baptism.

ii   This order forms part of the congregation's Sunday worship.

iii   At the conclusion of each prayer, the people say or sing **Amen**.

A Congregational Reaffirmation of Baptism

1   INTRODUCTION

2   REAFFIRMATION OF BAPTISM

The people stand.

Do you turn to Christ?

I turn to Christ.

Do you repent of your sins?

I repent of my sins.

Do you renounce evil
and the false values of this world?

I renounce them.

And now I ask you to confess the faith
into which you were baptised,
and in which you continue to live and grow:

Do you believe in God,
who made you and loves you?

**I believe in God, the Father almighty,
    creator of heaven and earth.**

Do you believe in Jesus Christ,
your Saviour and Lord?

I believe in Jesus Christ, God's only Son, our Lord,
who was conceived by the Holy Spirit,
born of the Virgin Mary,
suffered under Pontius Pilate,
was crucified, died, and was buried;
he descended to the dead.
On the third day he rose again;
he ascended into heaven,
he is seated at the right hand of the Father,
and he will come to judge the living and the dead.

Do you believe in the Holy Spirit,
and the continuing work of our salvation?

I believe in the Holy Spirit,
the holy catholic Church,
the communion of saints,
the forgiveness of sins,
the resurrection of the body,
and the life everlasting. Amen.

This is the faith of God's baptised people.

We are not ashamed to confess it
in Christ our Lord.

I ask you now to pledge yourselves
to Christ's ministry in the world:

Will you continue in the community of faith,
the apostles' teaching,
the breaking of bread and the prayers?

With God's help, we will.

Will you proclaim by word and example
the good news of God in Christ?

With God's help, we will.

Will you seek Christ in all people,
and love your neighbour as yourself?

With God's help, we will.

Will you strive for justice and peace,
and respect the dignity of every human being?

With God's help, we will.

May almighty God,
who has given us new birth by water and the Holy Spirit,
keep us steadfast in the faith,
and bring us to eternal life;
through Jesus Christ our Lord.
Amen.

3   RECOLLECTION OF BAPTISM

The people remain standing.

An elder pours water into the font.

The elder then says:

Come, Lord Jesus,
refresh the lives of all your faithful people.

The minister says one or more of the following; and may sprinkle water from the font by hand three times towards the people:

Always remember you are baptised,
and be thankful.

and/or

Always remember you are baptised,
and give thanks to the risen Lord.

and/or

Always remember you are baptised,
and praise the Holy Spirit.

The minister may then say:

Today we remember that, from the time of our baptism,
the sign of the cross has been upon us.
I invite you now to join me
in tracing the sign of the cross upon your forehead,
saying — I belong to Christ. Amen.

The minister and people may mark themselves with the sign, saying:

I belong to Christ. Amen.

The minister may also add:

You may trace the sign of the cross
on those around you,
saying — You belong to Christ. Amen.

The people may mark others with the sign, saying:

You belong to Christ. Amen.

4 HYMN

At the conclusion of the hymn, the people sit.

5 OFFERING

6 NOTICES AND CONCERNS OF THE CHURCH

7 PRAYERS OF THE PEOPLE

Let us pray for all the baptised everywhere
and for ourselves in this congregation of God's people:

That our redemption from evil
and our rescue from the way of sin and death
may be evident in our daily living:
Lord, in your mercy,
hear our prayer.

That the Holy Spirit may continue
to open our hearts and lives
to the grace and truth we find in Jesus our Lord:
Lord, in your mercy,
hear our prayer.

That we may be kept in the faith and communion
of the holy, catholic and apostolic Church:
Lord, in your mercy,
hear our prayer.

That we may be sent into the world
to witness to the love of Christ:
Lord, in your mercy,
hear our prayer.

That we may be brought to the fullness
of God's peace and glory:
Lord, in your mercy,
hear our prayer.

Other prayers for the peoples of the world, for the nation and the
community, and for situations of need are offered.

To conclude the prayers, the following prayer of commitment may
be said by all the people:

**Praise be to you, my Lord Jesus Christ,
for all the benefits
you have won for me,
for all the pains and insults
you have borne for me.**

**O most merciful Redeemer,
friend and brother,
may I know you more clearly,
love you more dearly,
and follow you more nearly,
day by day. Amen.**

Attributed to St Richard of Chichester

8   THE PEACE

The people stand for the greeting of peace.

The minister says:

We are the body of Christ.
In the one Spirit we were all baptised into one body.
Let us then pursue all that makes for peace
and builds up our common life.

The peace of the Lord be always with you.
And also with you.

The people may exchange a sign of peace.

The Sacrament of the Lord's Supper

The service continues from page 64 in The Service of the Lord's Day.

A Personal Reaffirmation
of Baptism

NOTES

i   This service witnesses to the fact that the Holy Spirit given in baptism has awakened a response of faith in a person's life. It may be used to meet particular situations such as the following:

- When a baptised and confirmed member of a congregation has come into a renewing and transforming experience of the love of Christ, and desires to witness to this experience before his/her congregation.

- When a baptised and confirmed member has lapsed from faith and active involvement in the life of a congregation of the Uniting Church or other denomination of the church, and now desires to reaffirm allegiance to Christ.

ii   This order forms part of the congregation's Sunday worship.

iii   At the conclusion of each prayer, the people say or sing **Amen**.

A Personal Reaffirmation of Baptism

1   INTRODUCTION AND WELCOME

N, why have you come here today?

I have come to reaffirm my baptism,
and to ask the congregation to pray for me.

The minister welcomes the person, and says:

We rejoice that today N has come
to give witness to the gracious gift of God in salvation,
and with renewed faith to commit his/her life
to the service of the Lord and the work of the church.

In our baptism we die and are raised to life
through the death and resurrection of Christ.
We are made members of the family of God
and live under the lordship of Christ.

Despite our unfaithfulness,
God is always faithful,
and through the Holy Spirit reawakens faith,
leading us into new awareness
of the salvation offered in Christ.

2   WITNESS

3   CONGREGATIONAL RESPONSE

The elder may make a brief response to the witness, concluding with:

N, we rejoice in your acknowledgment
of the work of Christ in your life.
He has opened your ears to receive God's word
and your mouth to proclaim his praise.

**In the love of Christ we encourage you,
and pray that he will continue to bless you.
To his name be glory and praise.
Hallelujah!**

4   HYMN

5   BAPTISMAL CANDLE

6   REAFFIRMATION OF BAPTISM

N, through your baptism you entered the covenant
which God has established with his people.

I invite you now to reaffirm your baptism
by giving answer to these questions:

Do you turn again to Christ?

I turn to Christ.

Do you repent of your sins?

I repent of my sins.

Do you renounce evil
and the false values of this world?

I renounce them.

Let us all confess the faith
into which we were baptised,
and in which we continue to live and grow:

I believe in God, the Father almighty,
 creator of heaven and earth.

I believe in Jesus Christ, God's only Son, our Lord,
 who was conceived by the Holy Spirit,
 born of the Virgin Mary,
 suffered under Pontius Pilate,
 was crucified, died, and was buried;
 he descended to the dead.
 On the third day he rose again;
 he ascended into heaven,
 he is seated at the right hand of the Father,
 and he will come to judge the living and the dead.

I believe in the Holy Spirit,
 the holy catholic Church,
 the communion of saints,
 the forgiveness of sins,
 the resurrection of the body,
 and the life everlasting. Amen.

The person places the lighted baptismal candle in an empty candle
holder on the communion table.

The people sit.

7 PRAYER WITH THE LAYING ON OF HANDS

Some of the congregation, family and friends who have been invited come forward to lay hands on the person's head.

Prayers are offered.

The people may say or sing the Aaronic Blessing, *(Australian Hymn Book, 572)*.

**The Lord bless you and keep you;
the Lord make his face to shine upon you,
and be gracious unto you;
the Lord lift up his countenance upon you,
and give you peace.**

Numbers 6:24-26

8 INVITATION TO DISCIPLESHIP

9 HYMN

10 OFFERING

11 NOTICES AND CONCERNS OF THE CHURCH

12 PRAYERS OF THE PEOPLE

13 THE PEACE

The people stand for the greeting of peace.

The minister says:

We are the body of Christ.
In the one Spirit we were all baptised into one body.
Let us then pursue all that makes for peace
and builds up our common life.

The peace of the Lord be always with you.
And also with you.

The people may exchange a sign of peace.

The Sacrament of the Lord's Supper

The service continues from page 64 in The Service of the Lord's Day.

The Covenant Service

NOTES

This service is intended for occasional use by the whole congregation.
The first Sunday of the New Year, the Sunday on which church activities
recommence after the summer holidays, the church anniversary or any
other significant occasion in the life of the congregation is an
appropriate time for renewing the covenant with God.

The Covenant Service

The Gathering of the People of God

1   CALL TO WORSHIP

Come, let us worship God,
who has called us to be a holy people,
and has established an everlasting covenant
through Jesus Christ our Lord.

We come in spirit and in truth.

2   ADORATION

A hymn of adoration and/or the following prayer, based on 'We praise you, O God' (*Te Deum Laudamus*), is used:

Let us pray:

Let us adore the God of love:
who created us;
who continually preserves and sustains us;
who has loved us with an everlasting love,
and given us the light of the knowledge of his glory
in the face of Jesus Christ.

**We praise you, O God,
we acclaim you as Lord.**

Let us glory in the grace of our Lord Jesus Christ:
though he was rich, yet for our sakes he became poor;
he was tempted in all points as we are, yet without sin;
he went about doing good
and preaching the gospel of the kingdom;
he became obedient to death, death on the cross;
he was dead and is alive for evermore;
he has opened the kingdom of heaven to all believers;

he is seated at God's right hand in glory;
he will come again to be our judge.
You are the king of glory, O Christ.
Let us rejoice in the fellowship of the Holy Spirit,
the Lord, the giver of life:
whose witness confirms us;
whose wisdom teaches us;
whose power enables us.
By the Spirit we are born into the family of God,
and made members of Christ's body.
All praise to you, O Holy Spirit.

3 CONFESSION

Let us humbly confess our sins to God:
Merciful God,
you have set forth the way of life for us
in your beloved Son.
We confess with shame our slowness to learn of him,
our failure to follow him,
our reluctance to bear the cross.
Have mercy on us, Lord, and forgive us.

or

Lord, have mercy. *(sung)*
We confess the poverty of our worship,
our neglect of the christian community
and of the means of grace,
our hesitating witness for Christ,
our evasion of responsibilities in your service,
our imperfect stewardship of your gifts.
Have mercy on us, Lord, and forgive us.

or

Christ, have mercy. *(sung)*

We confess that so little of your love
has reached others through us;
that we have cherished things
which divide us from others;
that we have made it hard for others to live with us;
that we have been thoughtless in our judgments,
hasty in condemnation,
and grudging in forgiveness.

Have mercy on us, Lord, and forgive us.

or

Lord, have mercy. *(sung)*

Let each of us in silence make confession to God.

After a time the minister says:

This is the message we have heard from Christ
and proclaim to you,
that God is light and in him is no darkness at all.
If we walk in the light, as God is in the light,
we have fellowship with one another,
and the blood of Jesus his Son cleanses us from all sin.
If we say we have no sin,
we deceive ourselves, and the truth is not in us.
If we confess our sins,
God is faithful and just, and will forgive our sins
and cleanse us from all unrighteousness.

1 John 1:5, 7-9

Hear then Christ's word of grace to us:
Your sins are forgiven.

Thanks be to God.

4   COLLECT

Almighty God,
you have appointed our Lord Jesus Christ
as mediator of a New Covenant.
Give us grace to draw near with full assurance of faith,
and rejoice in our continuing covenant with you;
through Christ your Son.
Amen.

5   HYMN

The Service of the Word

6   FIRST READING

Jeremiah 31:31-34, or the lectionary reading for the day, or other
appropriate reading.

7   PSALM

8   SECOND READING

Hebrews 12:22-24, or the lectionary reading for the day, or other
appropriate reading.

9   GOSPEL

John 15:1-11, or the lectionary reading for the day, or other
appropriate reading.

The following may be used after this final reading:

This is the word of the Lord.
Thanks be to God.

10 HYMN

11 PREACHING OF THE WORD

After the preaching, silence may be kept for meditation.

12 OFFERING

13 NOTICES AND CONCERNS OF THE CHURCH

14 PRAYERS OF THE PEOPLE

15 HYMN

The Covenant

16 INTRODUCTION

In the Old Covenant,
God chose Israel as his people
and gave them the gift of the Law.
In the New Covenant,
he made the gift of his Son Jesus Christ,
who fulfils the Law for us.
We stand within the New Covenant
and we bear the name of Christ.

God promises us new life in him.
We receive this promise
and pledge to live not for ourselves but for God.
This covenant is renewed each time we meet
at the table of the Lord.

Today we meet, as generations before us have met,
to renew that which bound them and now binds us to God.

The people stand.

Beloved in Christ,
let us again claim this covenant for ourselves,
and take the yoke of Christ upon us.

To take his yoke upon us means that we are content
that he appoint us our place and work,
and that he himself be our reward.

Christ has many services to be done:
some are easy, others are difficult;
some bring honour, others bring reproach;
some are suitable to our natural inclinations
and material interests,
others are contrary to both.
In some we may please Christ and please ourselves;
in others we cannot please Christ
except by denying ourselves.
Yet the power to do all these things
is given us in Christ, who strengthens us.

Therefore let us make this covenant with God our own,
trusting in the eternal promises
and relying on divine grace.

17 THE COVENANT PRAYER

Let us pray:

Lord God,
in baptism you brought us into union with Christ
who fulfils your gracious covenant;
and in bread and wine
we receive the fruit of his obedience.
So with joy
we take upon ourselves the yoke of obedience,
and commit ourselves to seek and do your perfect will.

I am no longer my own, but yours.

**I am no longer my own, but yours.
Put me to what you will,
rank me with whom you will;
put me to doing, put me to suffering;
let me be employed for you or laid aside for you;
exalted for you or brought low for you;
let me be full, let me be empty;
let me have all things, let me have nothing;
I freely and wholeheartedly yield all things
to your pleasure and disposal.**

**And now, glorious and blessed God,
Father, Son and Holy Spirit,
you are mine and I am yours,
to the glory and praise of your name. Amen.**

18 THE PEACE

The minister says:

We are the body of Christ.
The Spirit is with us.

The peace of the Lord be always with you.
And also with you.

The people may exchange a sign of peace.

The Sacrament of the Lord's Supper

The service continues from page 64 at 17 HYMN in The Service of the Lord's Day.

The Service of the Lord's Day

The Service of the Lord's Day

NOTES

i   Christian worship is God's gift whereby we participate through the Spirit in the Son's communion with the Father. Thus we are called as the people of God, with the gifts the Spirit has distributed among us, to take part in what Christ, our one Mediator and High Priest has done and continues to do for us. So the bread which we break is a participation in the body of Christ and the cup we take is a participation in the blood of Christ.

ii   Since New Testament times, the Lord's people have gathered at the Lord's table on the Lord's day. This is to remember Christ's death and resurrection and to celebrate the sacraments as signs of the last day, the day of consummation. Through the ages the basic structure of christian worship has remained the same. In Reformed practice, despite variations for historical reasons, this pattern has been maintained.

iii   The following order of service reflects this basic structure and may be used whether or not the eucharist is celebrated. When the section entitled 'The Sacrament of the Lord's Supper' is omitted, other acts of thanksgiving and dedication are used.

iv   This service has four parts:

The Gathering of the People of God
Summoned by God's good news, we come together to offer our praise to God, to confess the grace of our Lord Jesus Christ in the forgiveness of sin, and to hear God's word.

The Service of the Word
The Scriptures of the Old and New Testaments are read and proclaimed; and in grateful response we make an offering of faith in a creed, an offering of our concern for others in prayers of intercession, and an offering of money as our participation in the mission of Christ in the whole world.

The Sacrament of the Lord's Supper

God feeds his baptised people in the Spirit with the body and blood of Christ. In the breaking of the bread, the church acknowledges the presence of Christ, who re-presents himself to his disciples as the risen crucified One. In communion with Christ, we make our sacrifice of praise and thanksgiving and proclaim the Lord's death until he comes.

The Sending Forth of the People of God

Having been nourished, we are drawn into Christ's mission in the world, and God sends us forth in the power of the Spirit to love and serve all people.

v   At the conclusion of each prayer, the people say or sing: **Amen.**

Prayers Before the Service

The following prayers may be used privately by the people as they prepare for the service, or with the leaders of worship in the vestry. They may also be used during the service.

A

Lord Jesus Christ,
by your Holy Spirit
be present with us now. Amen.

B

Almighty God,
to whom all hearts are open,
all desires known,
and from whom no secrets are hidden:
cleanse the thoughts of our hearts
by the inspiration of your Holy Spirit,
that we may perfectly love you,
and worthily magnify your holy name;
through Christ our Lord. Amen.

C

O Lord our God,
you have given your word
to be a lamp to our feet and a light to our path.
Grant us grace to receive your truth in faith and love,
that we may be obedient to your will
and live always for your glory;
through Jesus Christ our Lord. Amen.

D
Be present, risen Lord Jesus,
as you were with your disciples,
and make yourself known to us
in the breaking of the bread;
for you live and reign with the Father and the Holy Spirit,
one God, for ever and ever. Amen.

E
We do not presume
to come to your table, merciful Lord,
trusting in our own righteousness,
but in your manifold and great mercies.
We are not worthy
so much as to gather up the crumbs under your table.
But you are the same Lord
whose nature is always to have mercy.
Grant us, therefore, gracious Lord,
so to eat the flesh of your dear Son Jesus Christ,
and to drink his blood,
that we may evermore dwell in him,
and he in us. Amen.

A Service of Word and Sacrament

The Gathering of the People of God

The people may stand as the open Bible is carried in and placed on the lectern or pulpit.

1 CALL TO WORSHIP

2 HYMN

After the hymn, the people remain standing.

3 GREETING

The grace of the Lord Jesus Christ
and the love of God
and the fellowship of the Holy Spirit
be with you all.
And also with you.

2 Corinthians 13:14

The people sit.

A brief introduction to the theme of the service may be given.

4 PRAYERS OF ADORATION AND CONFESSION

Silence may be kept after an invitation to prayer.

A prayer of adoration is offered.

The people are called to confess their sins.

After a time of silence, one of the following forms may be used, or free prayer offered.

Let us pray:

Merciful God,
our maker and our judge,
we have sinned against you in thought, word, and deed:
we have not loved you with our whole heart,
we have not loved our neighbours as ourselves;
we repent, and are sorry for all our sins.
Father, forgive us.
Strengthen us to love and obey you in newness of life;
through Jesus Christ our Lord. Amen.

or

The following responses may be said or sung:

Let us pray:

The first petition is offered.

Lord, have mercy.
Lord, have mercy.

A second petition is offered.

Christ, have mercy.
Christ, have mercy.

A third petition is offered.

Lord, have mercy.
Lord, have mercy.

DECLARATION OF FORGIVENESS

After a Scripture sentence, the leader says:

Hear then Christ's word of grace to us:
Your sins are forgiven.
Thanks be to God.

5   DOXOLOGY

One of these doxologies may be said or sung,
the people standing:

**Glory to God in the highest,
and peace to God's people on earth.**

**Lord God, heavenly King,
almighty God and Father,
    we worship you, we give you thanks,
    we praise you for your glory.**

**Lord Jesus Christ, only Son of the Father,
Lord God, Lamb of God,
you take away the sin of the world:
    have mercy on us;
you are seated at the right hand of the Father:
    receive our prayer.**

**For you alone are the Holy One,
you alone are the Lord,
you alone are the Most High,
    Jesus Christ,
    with the Holy Spirit,
    in the glory of God the Father. Amen.**

or

**Now to him who loved us, gave us
every pledge that love could give,
freely shed his blood to save us,
gave his life that we might live,
be the kingdom
and dominion
and the glory evermore.**

A.H.B., 576

The Service of the Word

If a brief address is to be given to young people,
it is appropriate at this point or after a Scripture reading.

The address may be followed by a hymn or song.

A brief introduction may be given to the readings of the day.

Before the readings, a prayer for illumination or the collect of the
day may be offered, or the following may be said or sung:

Your word, O Lord, is a lamp to our feet:
a light to our path.

   6   FIRST READING

   7   PSALM

   8   SECOND READING

   9   GOSPEL

After the final reading, one of the following may be said or sung:

This is the word of the Lord.
Thanks be to God.

or

Lord, may your word live in us:
and bear much fruit to your glory.

  10   HYMN

11   PREACHING OF THE WORD

After the preaching, silence may be kept for meditation.

> *If there is no celebration of The Sacrament of the Lord's Supper, The Service of the Lord's Day continues on page 69.*

12   AFFIRMATION OF FAITH

A creed of the church may be said or sung.

The people stand.

We believe in one God,
   the Father, the Almighty,
   maker of heaven and earth,
   of all that is, seen and unseen.

We believe in one Lord, Jesus Christ,
   the only Son of God,
   eternally begotten of the Father,
   God from God, Light from Light,
   true God from true God,
   begotten, not made,
   of one Being with the Father;
   through him all things were made.
   For us and for our salvation
     he came down from heaven,
     was incarnate by the Holy Spirit of the Virgin Mary
     and became truly human.

For our sake he was crucified under Pontius Pilate;
he suffered death and was buried.
On the third day he rose again
in accordance with the Scriptures;
he ascended into heaven
and is seated at the right hand of the Father.
He will come again in glory
    to judge the living and the dead,
and his kingdom will have no end.

We believe in the Holy Spirit, the Lord, the giver of life,
who proceeds from the Father,
who with the Father and the Son
    is worshipped and glorified,
who has spoken through the prophets.
We believe in one holy catholic and apostolic Church.
We acknowledge one baptism for the forgiveness of sins.
We look for the resurrection of the dead,
    and the life of the world to come. Amen.

Nicene Creed

The people sit.

13   OFFERING

14   NOTICES AND CONCERNS OF THE CHURCH

15   PRAYERS OF THE PEOPLE

Prayers are offered for the church,
        for the peoples of the world,
        for the nation and the community,
        and for situations of need.

After each prayer the people may say or sing: **Amen.**

A response may be said or sung such as:

Lord, in your mercy,
hear our prayer.

or

Lord, hear us.
Lord, hear our prayer.

The prayers may conclude with
        a commemoration of the faithful departed,
        the collect of the day,
        or some other appropriate collect.

The Sacrament of the Lord's Supper

16   THE PEACE

The people stand for the greeting of peace.

The peace of the Lord be always with you.
And also with you.

The people may exchange a sign of peace.

17   HYMN

18   SETTING OF THE TABLE

19   GREAT PRAYER OF THANKSGIVING

> The Narrative of the Institution of the Lord's Supper either is
> read first or else forms part of the Great Prayer of Thanksgiving.
>
> The people stand.

The Lord be with you.
And also with you.

Lift up your hearts.
We lift them to the Lord.

Let us give thanks to the Lord our God.
It is right to give our thanks and praise.

> The Great Prayer of Thanksgiving begins, and after a time the
> minister and the people sing or say: 'Holy, holy, holy Lord …'

And so we praise you
with the faithful of every time and place,
joining with choirs of angels and the whole creation
in the eternal hymn:

**Holy, holy, holy Lord, God of power and might,
heaven and earth are full of your glory.**
  Hosanna in the highest.

Blessed is he who comes in the name of the Lord.
  Hosanna in the highest.

> The Great Prayer of Thanksgiving continues, concluding with
> an ascription of glory to God to which the people respond:
> **Amen.**

THE LORD'S PRAYER

Our Father in heaven,
  hallowed be your name,
  your kingdom come,
  your will be done,
    on earth as in heaven.
Give us today our daily bread.
Forgive us our sins
  as we forgive those who sin against us.
Save us from the time of trial
  and deliver us from evil.

For the kingdom, the power, and the glory are yours
  now and for ever. Amen.

The people sit.

20   THE BREAKING OF THE BREAD

21   LAMB OF GOD

Jesus, Lamb of God,
  have mercy on us.

Jesus, bearer of our sins,
  have mercy on us.

Jesus, redeemer of the world,
  grant us peace.

or

Lamb of God, you take away the sin of the world,
  have mercy on us.

Lamb of God, you take away the sin of the world,
  have mercy on us.

Lamb of God, you take away the sin of the world,
  grant us peace.

22   THE COMMUNION

Words such as the following are said before or during the
distribution:

The body of Christ, given for you.
Amen.

and

The blood of Christ, given for you.
Amen.

or

The body of Christ keep you in eternal life.
Amen.

and

The blood of Christ keep you in eternal life.
Amen.

After all have received, a time of silence may be kept.

23   PRAYER AFTER COMMUNION

The Sending Forth of the People of God

24 HYMN

25 WORD OF MISSION

26 BLESSING

May almighty God bless you,
the Father, the Son and the Holy Spirit.
Amen.

or

The blessing of God almighty,
the Father, the Son and the Holy Spirit,
be upon you and remain with you always.
Amen.

27 DISMISSAL

The following dismissal may be given:

Go in peace to love and serve the Lord.
In the name of Christ. Amen.

*If there is no celebration of The Sacrament of the
Lord's Supper, The Service of the Lord's Day
continues from here.*

12   AFFIRMATION OF FAITH

The people stand.

13   HYMN

14   OFFERING

15   NOTICES AND CONCERNS OF THE CHURCH

16   PRAYERS OF THE PEOPLE

Prayers of thanksgiving and intercession are offered.

The intercessions may include prayers
for the church,
for the peoples of the world,
for the nation and the community,
and for situations of need.

After each prayer, the people may say or sing: **Amen.**

A response may be said or sung such as:

Lord, in your mercy,
hear our prayer.

or

Lord, hear us.
Lord, hear our prayer.

The prayers may conclude with
a commemoration of the faithful departed,
the collect of the day,
or some other appropriate collect.

THE LORD'S PRAYER

**Our Father in heaven,
hallowed be your name,
your kingdom come,
your will be done,
on earth as in heaven.
Give us today our daily bread.
Forgive us our sins
as we forgive those who sin against us.
Save us from the time of trial
and deliver us from evil.**

**For the kingdom, the power, and the glory are yours
now and for ever. Amen.**

The Sending Forth of the People of God

17   HYMN

18   WORD OF MISSION

19   BLESSING

May almighty God bless you,
the Father, the Son and the Holy Spirit.
Amen.

or

The blessing of God almighty,
the Father, the Son and the Holy Spirit,
be upon you and remain with you always.
Amen.

20   DISMISSAL

Go in peace to love and serve the Lord.
In the name of Christ. Amen.

Communion Beyond
the Gathered Congregation

NOTES

i   It is important that church members should not be deprived of hearing the Word and receiving holy communion because sickness or some other reason prevents them from joining in Sunday worship with the congregation.

ii   Normally, during a pastoral visit to such people, the minister will give communion, using a brief but complete order of service. However, in some parishes the minister and elders may decide to allow elders or other lay people appointed by the council of elders to take some of the bread and wine from the communion in the church to people at home or in hospital after the service. This order of service is designed for such use.

iii   Wherever possible, this ministry should take place on the Sunday and is to be regarded as part of the worship of the whole congregation. It would be appropriate to read one of the Bible readings used in the congregation (or at least some of the verses from that reading) and for the visitor to share some points from the sermon.

iv   The length of the service and what is to be included will depend on the situation of the person(s) visited. In some cases of sickness brevity is essential. For some housebound people their sense of isolation is eased by sharing in a longer service.

v   Prior arrangements should be made for each visit. Before the first such visit to any person(s), the purpose of the service and the procedure to be followed should be explained and the person(s) given the opportunity to accept or reject this form of ministry.

vi   The minister should prepare the visitors for this ministry. Spiritual preparation for conducting the service and general advice about visiting can be offered. The minister may also want to suggest the Bible reading to be used and points to be included in the Reflection and Prayers.

vii Care should be taken that the bread and wine are taken in adequate containers and can be served in an appropriate manner. Following the visit, or the last visit if a series of calls is made on the day, any remaining bread or wine should be consumed or otherwise disposed of in a reverent manner.

viii It would be appropriate for the congregation to know who are to be visited with the communion and who are to make the visits. All these can be remembered in the prayers of the congregation.

Communion Beyond the Gathered Congregation

GREETING

The grace of the Lord Jesus Christ
and the love of God
and the fellowship of the Holy Spirit
be with you.
And also with you.

2 Corinthians 13:14

PRAYER

The elder or other lay person may offer free prayer.

The theme of the prayer(s) may include the invocation and adoration of God and the confession of sin.

BIBLE READING

The theme of the day may be introduced and/or one of the readings of the day may be used.

REFLECTION

A brief reflection on the reading or a brief summary of the preaching in the congregation may be given.

PRAYERS OF THE PEOPLE

Greetings from the congregation and news of the congregation may be given.

Prayers of intercession may be offered here or during the Prayer after Communion.

The prayers may include intercessions for the church and the world, for the home or hospital and the person(s) being visited, and for the congregation.

The collect of the day and/or the Lord's Prayer may conclude
Prayers of the People.

Our Father in heaven,
hallowed be your name,
your kingdom come,
your will be done,
on earth as in heaven.
Give us today our daily bread.
Forgive us our sins
as we forgive those who sin against us.
Save us from the time of trial
and deliver us from evil.

For the kingdom, the power, and the glory are yours
now and for ever. Amen.

or

Our Father, who art in heaven,
hallowed be thy name,
thy kingdom come,
thy will be done
on earth as it is in heaven.
Give us this day our daily bread.
And forgive us our trespasses,
as we forgive those who trespass against us.
And lead us not into temptation,
but deliver us from evil.

For thine is the kingdom, the power and the glory,
for ever and ever. Amen.

RECEPTION OF COMMUNION

The elder or other lay person says:

In obedience to the Lord Jesus,
our congregation has shared today in holy communion,
as christians have done through the ages.

This bread and this wine
have been brought from the communion table
so that you also may receive Christ's body and blood,
and be nourished for eternal life.

So let us lift our hearts to the Lord,
and receive this sacrament with thanksgiving.

The following prayer may be said together, or by the leader only.

Let us pray:

**Father, we thank you
that you feed us in these holy mysteries
with the spiritual food
of the body and blood of our Saviour, Jesus Christ.
We thank you for this assurance
of your goodness and love,
and that we are living members of his body
and heirs of his eternal kingdom.
May the Holy Spirit be upon us now,
that as we receive this bread and wine
we may know the presence and power
of Christ our Lord. Amen.**

The following is said with the giving of the bread:

The body of Christ, given for you.
Amen.

or

The body of Christ keep you in eternal life.
Amen.

The following is said with the giving of the cup:

The blood of Christ, given for you.
Amen.

or

The blood of Christ keep you in eternal life.
Amen.

PRAYER AFTER COMMUNION

After a time of silence, a prayer of thanksgiving and commitment may be offered.

THE PEACE

The peace of the Lord be always with you.
And also with you.

A sign of peace may be exchanged.

BLESSING

The blessing of God almighty,
the Father, the Son and the Holy Spirit,
be upon us and remain with us always.
Amen.

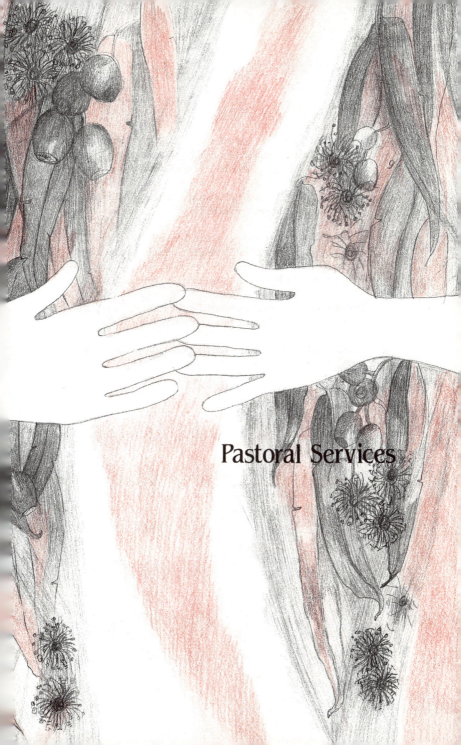

Pastoral Services

NOTES

i   The christian celebration of marriage is an act of worship, an expression of the church's offering of the whole of life to God. It is a pastoral occasion in which the community of faith shares in the joy of bridegroom and bride. It is also an evangelical occasion in which all those who have come to witness the marriage may be challenged by the implications of the christian faith.

ii   Normally a marriage is to be celebrated in a church. Lay people, particularly family members, attendants and close friends, are encouraged to share in the leadership of the service. The reading of Scripture and the Prayers lend themselves to this purpose.

iii   Holy communion may be included in the wedding service if both bridegroom and bride are regular communicants.

iv   At the conclusion of each prayer, the people say or sing **Amen**.

The Marriage Service

The Gathering of the Community

1   GREETING

Grace to you and peace
from God our Father and the Lord Jesus Christ.

Romans 1:7

Amen.

or

The Lord be with you.
And also with you.

We have come together in the presence of God
to witness the marriage of
NNN
and NNN,
to surround them with our prayers,
and to share in their joy.

2   SCRIPTURE SENTENCES

3   HYMN

After the hymn, the people sit.

4   DECLARATION OF PURPOSE

The minister reminds the couple and the congregation of God's
purpose for marriage.

The Service of the Word

5 SCRIPTURE READINGS

This is the word of the Lord.
Thanks be to God.

6 SERMON

The Marriage

7 PRAYER

8 DECLARATION OF INTENT

> The minister asks the couple the questions about their
> understanding of marriage and their willingness to be married to
> each other.

9 AFFIRMATION BY THE FAMILIES

10 AFFIRMATION BY THE PEOPLE

Will you, the families and friends of N and N,
who have come to share this wedding day,
uphold them in their marriage?

We will.

11 THE VOWS

Both the bridegroom and bride make their marriage vows.

12 GIVING OF THE RINGS

13 PROCLAMATION OF THE MARRIAGE

The people stand.

The Blessing of the Marriage

14 ACCLAMATIONS

Blessed are you, heavenly Father:
You give joy to bridegroom and bride.

Blessed are you, Lord Jesus Christ:
You have brought new life to the world.

Blessed are you, Holy Spirit of God:
You bring us together in love.

Blessed be Father, Son and Holy Spirit:
One God to be praised for ever. Amen.

15 BLESSING

16 THE PEACE

The minister gives the greeting of peace:

The peace of the Lord be always with you.
And also with you.

Signs of peace may be exchanged.

The people sit.

17 PRAYERS

The minister and/or lay person(s) leads the people in prayer.

Each petition or group of petitions may conclude with:

Lord, hear us,
Lord, hear our prayer.

18 THE LORD'S PRAYER

**Our Father in heaven,
  hallowed be your name,
  your kingdom come,
  your will be done,
    on earth as in heaven.
Give us today our daily bread.
Forgive us our sins
  as we forgive those who sin against us.
Save us from the time of trial
  and deliver us from evil.**

**For the kingdom, the power, and the glory are yours
  now and for ever. Amen.**

or

Our Father, who art in heaven,
hallowed be thy name,
thy kingdom come,
thy will be done
    on earth as it is in heaven.
Give us this day our daily bread.
And forgive us our trespasses,
    as we forgive those who trespass against us.
And lead us not into temptation,
    but deliver us from evil.

For thine is the kingdom, the power and the glory,
    for ever and ever. Amen.

19 HOLY COMMUNION

Holy communion may be celebrated.

20 HYMN

At the conclusion, the people remain standing.

21 BLESSING

The blessing of God almighty,
the Father, the Son and the Holy Spirit,
be upon you and remain with you always.
Amen.

22 SIGNING OF THE MARRIAGE CERTIFICATES

NOTES

i   This service is intended for use when parents desire to give thanks to God in a service of worship for the birth or adoption of a child.

ii   This order should be used soon after the child's birth or adoption, regardless of whether or not the parents intend to present their child for baptism at a later date.

iii   At the conclusion of each prayer, the people say or sing **Amen**.

Thanksgiving for the Gift of a Child

1   HYMN

2   PRESENTATION

The elder responsible for the care of the family brings the
parent(s), the child and any brothers and sisters forward and
introduces them to the congregation.

Friends,
I present to you N and N
who have come to give thanks for their child N.
(I also present N and N
who are so glad to be welcoming
a new brother/sister into their family.)
With them, we give our thanks to God.

3   INTRODUCTION

All life is from God,
and children are a gift from the Lord.
Within a family,
the birth/adoption of a child
is a joyous and solemn occasion.
In this event we see the wonder
of God's loving creativity among us.

We are now to share the joy of this family
whose life has been enriched
by the gift of a son/daughter.

4 PSALM

Bless the Lord, O my soul,
    and all that is within me, bless his holy name.

Bless the Lord, O my soul,
    and forget not all his benefits.

He satisfies you with good things,
    and your youth is renewed like an eagle's.

As a father cares for his children,
    so does the Lord care for those who fear him.

The merciful goodness of the Lord endures for ever
on those who fear him,
    and his righteousness on children's children.

On those who keep his covenant
    and remember his commandments and do them.

Bless the Lord, all you works of his,
in all places of his dominion;
    bless the Lord, O my soul.

Psalm 103: 1, 2, 5, 13, 17, 18, 22

5 PRAYER OF THANKSGIVING

6   STATEMENT BY PARENTS

One or both parents may say one of the following:

**We thankfully receive N
as a gift from God.
With humility and hope
we promise to love and care for him/her.**

or

**We thankfully receive N
as a gift from God.
With humility and hope
we promise to love and care for him/her,
and to set before him/her the christian faith
by teaching and example.
In this we ask for the power of the Holy Spirit
and the prayers of the church.**

7   PRAYER

8   BLESSING

NOTES

i   Services of healing are of various kinds. The rite of healing may be
    included in The Service of the Lord's Day in response to a particular
    need within the congregation. Or the rite of healing may be given
    emphasis on a particular Sunday and a general invitation made for
    anyone in need of healing to come forward. In either of these cases,
    The Sacrament of the Lord's Supper may be included in the order of
    worship. The Service of Healing may be before or after communion.

    Special services of healing may be held at times other than the regular
    Sunday service of the congregation. Again, holy communion may be
    celebrated. The order should always include The Gathering of the
    People of God (including an act of confession) and The Service of the
    Word (including the Prayers of the People).

    A Service of Healing may also be conducted in a home or hospital
    for one who is unable to attend a service with the congregation. Some
    representatives of the congregation may be present with the minister. In
    these circumstances, with sensitive regard to a person's condition, the
    service may be considerably shortened.

ii The laying on of hands has always been a sign of blessing. It has from
    early times been closely associated with prayers for healing.

iii Anointing with oil has been a practice of the church from the
    beginning. (James 5:14) It is a sign of God's presence through the Holy
    Spirit and of the joy of those who welcome God. The anointing for
    healing is a solemn moment in anyone's life. Normally it is not used
    more than once for a particular illness, whereas the laying on of hands
    may be requested frequently for growth towards wholeness.

iv At the conclusion of each prayer, the people say or sing **Amen**.

A Service of Healing

The Laying on of Hands with Prayer and Anointing

INTRODUCTION

INVITATION

SAVIOUR OF THE WORLD

Jesus, Saviour of the world,
come to us in your mercy;
we look to you to save and help us.

By your cross and your life laid down
you set your people free;
we look to you to save and help us.

When they were about to perish
you saved your disciples;
we look to you to come to our help.

In the greatness of your mercy,
loose us from our chains;
forgive the sins of all your people.

Make yourself known as our Saviour
and mighty Deliverer;
save and help us that we may praise you.

Come now and dwell with us,
Lord Christ Jesus;
hear our prayer and be with us always.

And when you come in your glory,
  **make us to be one with you
  and to share the life of your kingdom.**

A: For the Healing of the Sick or Disabled

PRAYERS OF INTERCESSION

Those who wish to receive the laying on of hands come forward.

General prayers are offered for the sick and disabled, and prayers
for the healing of particular people.

THE LAYING ON OF HANDS

The minister lays hands on the sick person.

Others may also lay their hands on the person.

The minister says:

We lay our hands upon you, N,
in the name of our Lord Jesus Christ.

There may be a time of silence or free prayer.

The minister continues:

May almighty God,
the Father, the Son and the Holy Spirit,
bring you to wholeness in body, mind and spirit,
give you a secure hope and a confident peace,
and keep you in eternal life.
Amen.

THE ANOINTING

N, we anoint you with oil
for cleansing and healing
in the name of our Lord Jesus Christ.

May the Holy Spirit poured out upon you
yield the fruit of pardon, trust and joy.
Amen.

B: For the Healing of a Personal Relationship

PRAYERS OF INTERCESSION

THE LAYING ON OF HANDS

We lay our hands upon you, N (and N),
in the name of our Lord Jesus Christ.

The minister continues:

May almighty God,
the Father, the Son and the Holy Spirit,
who has broken down the barriers of hostility
and who calls us to live reconciled lives,
enable you to live in unity and peace.
Amen.

THE ANOINTING

If anointing is to take place, the minister makes the sign of the
cross with oil on the person(s).

The minister says:

N (and N), we anoint you with oil
for cleansing and healing
in the name of our Lord Jesus Christ.

The minister may add:

May the Holy Spirit poured out upon you
yield the fruit of pardon, trust and joy.
Amen.

C: For Healing Within Society

PRAYERS OF INTERCESSION

Conclusion

A prayer such as the following concludes A Service of Healing:

May almighty God,
the source of new life,
be your strong defence against discouragement and fear,
and kindle in your heart a sense of continuing healing;
through the One who brings salvation
and keeps you in eternal life,
Jesus Christ our Lord.
Amen.

The Service of the Lord's Day may continue at The Sacrament of
the Lord's Supper or The Sending Forth of the People of God. A
shorter form of service may conclude simply with a blessing.

NOTES

i   This short order is recommended for those occasions when it seems appropriate for a person to be reconciled to God in the presence of a representative of the whole church, normally a minister. It may be used at the close of a counselling session when something has surfaced which needs to be dealt with in the context of a prayer for forgiveness.

ii The substance of a personal confession is never to be communicated outside the place and time where the confession is made. Those who are given the privilege and responsibility of hearing another person open himself or herself in confession should understand that the one who confesses comes with a trusting confidence and longing for reconciliation with God and with fellow human beings.

iii The one confessing may kneel. This simple gesture may help the person to express humility and trust in God. Care should always be taken to ensure that the minister does not take up a position that makes it appear as if the confession is being made *to* another person. It is being made *in the presence of* another who is also in need of reconciliation. The one who declares forgiveness does so as a servant of God. God alone forgives and makes whole.

A Service of Reconciliation

A Form of Personal Confession

ACT OF CONFESSION

The one making confession says:

Lord,
purify me with the fire of the Holy Spirit,
so that I may serve you
with a pure and trusting heart.

Silence may be kept for a time.

I confess to almighty God,
in the communion of saints in heaven and on earth,
and before you, my brother/sister,
that I have sinned.

Here, specific things for which forgiveness is sought may be confessed.

The minister may ask questions and speak words of encouragement.

The one making confession then says:

My sins weigh me down;
but my confidence is in the Lord Jesus Christ
who has taken upon himself the burden of our sin.

I ask you, my brother/sister,
to pray for me to the Lord our God.

Free prayer is offered.

DECLARATION OF FORGIVENESS

The minister says one or more Scripture sentences.

The minister says:

Our Lord Jesus Christ forgives your offences
and releases you from your burden of guilt.

By his authority,
I declare the forgiveness of your sins.

You are free:
in the name of the Father,
and of the Son,
and of the Holy Spirit.
Amen.

THE PEACE

Both stand.

The minister says:

God was in Christ, reconciling the world to himself,
not counting our trespasses against us,
and entrusting to us the message of reconciliation.
Let us therefore be ambassadors of Christ.

2 Corinthians 5:19, 20

The peace of the Lord be always with you.
And also with you.

A sign of peace may be exchanged.

A Celebration of New Beginnings in Faith

NOTES

i   This service witnesses to the fact that the Holy Spirit is constantly working in the lives of God's people, awakening faith and calling them to make a new beginning in their christian pilgrimage. It may be used to meet particular situations such as the following:

- When a person has recently come to faith in Christ and desires to celebrate the experience and witness to it before his/her congregation.

- When a person has recently made a recommitment of his/her life to Christ.

- When a person intends to return to active involvement in the worship and life of the congregation and/or to seek baptism or confirmation.

ii   This order forms part of the congregation's Sunday worship.

iii   At the conclusion of each prayer, the people say **Amen**.

A Celebration of New Beginnings in Faith

1   INTRODUCTION AND WELCOME

2   SCRIPTURE SENTENCES

3   WITNESS

4   CONGREGATIONAL RESPONSE

The elder or other appropriate person may make a brief response to the witness, concluding with:

N, we rejoice in your experience
of the grace of the Lord Jesus Christ,
the love of God,
and the fellowship of the Holy Spirit.

The people say:

**In the love of Christ we encourage you,
and pray that he will continue to bless you.
To his name be glory and praise.
Hallelujah!**

The elder may initiate applause.

5   HYMN

6   PRAYER WITH THE LAYING ON OF HANDS

Some of the congregation, family and friends who have been invited come forward to lay hands on the person's head.

Prayers are offered.

7   BLESSING

The Lord bless you and keep you;
the Lord make his face to shine upon you;
and be gracious unto you;
the Lord lift up his countenance upon you,
and give you peace.

Numbers 6:24-26

8   INVITATION TO DISCIPLESHIP

9   HYMN

NOTES

i   This service is to be used when a confirmed or baptised member joins a congregation by transfer from another congregation of the Uniting Church in Australia or from another denomination.

ii This order forms part of the congregation's Sunday worship.

iii No formal act is required for the reception of an adherent, but if a family is being received and includes adherents as well as baptised and/or confirmed members, it may be appropriate to include the adherents in the presentation to the congregation and the welcome.

Reception of a Member by Transfer

An elder brings forward the person to be received and says:

The Uniting Church in Australia
affirms that every member of the church
is engaged to confess the faith of Christ crucified
and to be his faithful servant.
In each congregation the members are to meet regularly
to hear God's Word,
to celebrate the sacraments,
to build one another up in love,
to share in the wider responsibilities of the church,
and to serve the world.

I present to you NN
to be received as a confirmed member of this congregation,
by transfer from the . . . congregation.

or

I present to you NN
to be received as a baptised member of this congregation,
by transfer from the . . . congregation.

If the person is a confirmed member, the minister asks:

N,
do you reaffirm your allegiance to Jesus Christ
as Saviour and Lord?

I do.

Do you accept membership in this congregation,
promising to share in the life and worship of the church?

I do.

Reception of a Member by Transfer

If the person is a baptised member, an adult or a child able to speak for himself/herself, the minister asks:

N,
do you accept membership in this congregation,
promising to share in the life and worship of the church?

I do.

If the person to be received is an infant or young child, the minister asks the parents or guardian:

N (and N),
do you accept membership for N in this congregation,
promising to enable and encourage him/her
to share in the life and worship of the church?

We do.

The minister asks the congregation:

Will you welcome N
into the fellowship of this congregation,
and will you offer him/her
your friendship and support?

We will.

A prayer may be offered.

The minister takes the hand of the new member and says:

N, as a sign of our welcome,
we give you the right hand of fellowship.

Representatives of the council of elders and the congregation come forward and greet the new member. One may speak words of welcome on behalf of the congregation.

Reception of a Member-in-Association

NOTES

i   This service is to be used when a member of another denomination who for the time being intends to participate in the life of a congregation of the Uniting Church in Australia is received as a member-in-association.

ii   This order forms part of the congregation's Sunday worship.

Reception of a Member-in-Association

An elder brings forward the person to be received and says:

The Uniting Church in Australia
provides for a member of another christian denomination
who, for the time being,
participates in the life of a congregation of this church
to become a member-in-association.
Such a member joins in the corporate life
of the Uniting Church
while retaining membership in his or her own denomination.

I present to you NN
to be received as a member-in-association
of this congregation.

The minister asks the person:

N,
do you reaffirm your allegiance to Jesus Christ
as Saviour and Lord?

I do.

Do you accept membership-in-association in this congregation,
promising to share in the life and worship of the church;
and accepting the way in which the Uniting Church in Australia
orders its own life,
without forsaking your own denomination?

I do.

The minister asks the congregation:

Will you welcome N
into the fellowship of this congregation;
and will you offer him/her
your friendship and support?

We will.

A prayer may be offered.

The minister takes the hand of the new member and says:

N, as a sign of our welcome,
we give you the right hand of fellowship.

Representatives of the council of elders and the congregation
come forward and greet the new member. One may speak words
of welcome on behalf of the congregation.

NOTES

This service is for the commissioning or the recommissioning of elders elected by a congregation, and forms part of that congregation's regular Sunday worship.

Commissioning of Elders

1   SENTENCES

There are diverse gifts:
but it is the same Spirit who gives them.

There are different ways of serving God:
but it is the same Lord who is served.

God works through people in different ways:
**but it is the same God
whose purpose is achieved through them all.**

Each one of us is given a gift by the Spirit:
and there is no gift without its corresponding service.

There is one ministry of Christ:
and in this ministry we all share.

Together we are the body of Christ:
and individually members of it.

*Based on 1 Corinthians 12:4ff.
and Basis of Union, para. 13*

2   PRESENTATION

The minister addresses the people:

The Uniting Church provides for the exercise
by men and women
of the gifts God bestows upon them
for the building up of the church.

Having sought the guidance of the Holy Spirit,
we are now to commission as elders
those whom we have elected to this ministry.

On behalf of the people of this congregation,
I present the following persons
to be *commissioned* or *recommissioned* as elders:

Brothers and sisters,

or

N and N,

the congregation has elected you
to serve Jesus Christ as elders.

The responsibilities of the council of elders include the following:

to share with the minister
in building up the congregation in faith and love;

to nurture the members in their growth in grace;

to visit regularly the members and adherents;

to share with the minister
in the conduct of worship
and the administration of the sacraments,
the spiritual oversight of the congregation,
and in christian education and evangelistic outreach;

to maintain the membership rolls of the congregation
and to exercise pastoral discipline;

to make recommendations to the parish council
concerning applicants for training for ministry.

3 THE VOWS

The minister asks the candidates:

Do you confess anew Jesus Christ as Lord?

I do.

Do you believe that you are called by God
through the church to this ministry?

I do.

Will you seek to live and work within the faith and unity
of the one holy catholic and apostolic Church?

I will

Do you adhere to the Basis of Union
of the Uniting Church in Australia?

I do.

Relying on God's grace,
do you promise to carry out the duties of your office?

I do.

The people stand.

The minister says:

Will you, the members of this congregation,
accept these brothers and sisters (*or*, N and N) as elders?

We will.

Will you encourage them in love
and support them in their ministry,
serving with them the one Lord Jesus Christ?

We will.

May God give you strength to fulfil these vows;
and to him be the glory
in the church and in Christ Jesus
from generation to generation for ever.
Amen.

The people sit.

4   ACT OF COMMISSIONING

Those appointed by the council of elders to join with the minister
in the laying on of hands come forward.

Prayers are offered.

Hands are laid on the head of each candidate in turn and the
minister says:

N, receive the Holy Spirit
for the ministry of elder.

The people respond:

Amen.

The Aaronic Blessing may be said or sung by the people,
(Australian Hymn Book, 572), or said by the minister.

**The Lord bless you and keep you;
the Lord make his face to shine upon you,
and be gracious unto you;
the Lord lift up his countenance upon you,
and give you peace.**

Numbers 6:24-26

5   DECLARATION

In the name of our Lord Jesus Christ,
I declare you to be elders
of the Uniting Church in Australia
in the . . . Congregation.

The people may applaud.

The minister and other elders give the right hand of fellowship to
the new elders.

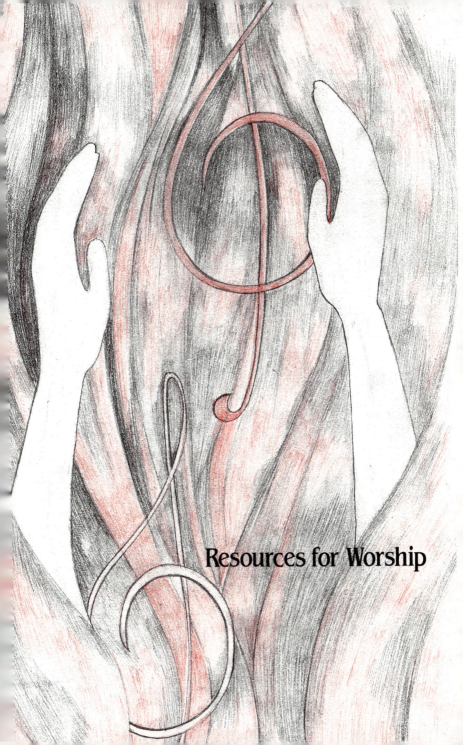

Resources for Worship

Resources for Worship

NOTES

These resources are arranged in seven groups:

   i   The Creeds of The Church

   ii   Statements of Faith

   iii   Canticles

   iv   Litanies

   v   Vestry Prayers

   vi   A Treasury of Prayers

   vii   Selections from The Psalter

I   The Creeds of The Church

When holy communion is celebrated, traditionally the Nicene Creed is used. This is the creed set out in The Service of the Lord's Day.

When baptism and/or confirmation is celebrated, the Apostles' Creed is included in the appropriate order. No other creed or statement of faith needs to be used at a service which includes the order for baptism and/or confirmation. The orders for A Congregational Reaffirmation of Baptism and A Personal Reaffirmation of Baptism also include the Apostles' Creed.

II   Statements of Faith

These include several passages from Scripture and a few contemporary statements of faith. One of these may be used in place of an historic creed if the service does not include the celebration of a sacrament.

Most of the statements are printed in standard type. These are intended to be said by both the leader of worship and the congregation in unison. Where bold type is also used, the leader of worship reads those parts printed in standard type and the congregation reads those parts in bold type.

III   Canticles

The word 'canticle', from the Latin *canticulum*, means 'a little song'. In the early church the word was used to describe a song from the Bible other than from the book of Psalms. These included many songs from the Old Testament, some of which are included in this selection. The three best known songs from the New Testament to which the word 'canticle' was applied are the Song of Mary, the Song of Zechariah and the Song of Simeon.

Later in the history of worship other songs of the early church were also called canticles. The best known of these are 'We praise you, O God', 'Glory to God in the highest' and 'Lamb of God'.

An extensive selection of other resources for worship has been included in this section. Most of them are of recent composition, although they draw on biblical imagery and language. While canticles are predominantly songs of praise, they also include the other great themes of christian devotion — confession, thanksgiving and intercession.

All the canticles are printed in a combination of both standard and bold type. Normally the leader of worship reads those parts in standard type and the congregation reads those parts in bold type. This may be varied. A short canticle such as the Song of Simeon may be said together by the leader of worship and the congregation. Or, if a canticle such as 'We praise you, O God' is being used as a statement of faith, it may be appropriate for the leader of worship and the congregation to read the first two sections in unison, and the third section responsively.

IV Litanies

A litany is a form of prayer in which the congregation makes responses to short biddings or petitions offered by the leader of worship. The use of the litany dates back to the worship of the early church and was firmly established as the normal way of offering intercessory prayer by the 5th century. During the week the litany was frequently included in the Services of the Hours and on Sundays it was generally used as a preparation for celebrating the Lord's supper.

The first litany in this selection, The Great Litany, represents the classical form of this method of praying. At the time of the Reformation it was shortened and adapted to that form which we find in the 1662 Book of Common Prayer. There are many modern adaptations of this.

Over the last few years, a considerable number of litanies has been written and published. Three of the litanies are designated 'Prayers of the People'; many others lend themselves for use by the leader of worship and the congregation at this part of The Service of the Lord's Day. If a litany is long, and particularly if it is divided into sections as in The Great Litany, it does not have to be used in its entirety at one time.

Many of the litanies in this section also lend themselves for the inclusion of free prayer. Contemporary and topical concerns may be woven into the appropriate stanzas by the use of free prayer. The leader of worship should introduce the free prayer into the earlier part of the stanza so that there is a return to the liturgical text in adequate time for the congregation to know when to read the response line.

A footnote at the conclusion of many of the litanies identifies the source of the prayer. The footnotes have been included in this section to remind us that there is an international and ecumenical fellowship of intercessory prayer for the church and the world.

V   **Vestry Prayers**

This selection of prayers is arranged in two groups:
(a)   Prayers with the minister or leader of worship, normally led by an elder or other lay person, in preparation for worship.

(b)   Prayers with the choir, normally led by the minister or leader of worship, in preparation for the service.

VI   **A Treasury of Prayers**

This selection is a small cross-section of christian prayers through the ages. It represents a rich heritage of devotion.

Prayers from this treasury may be found helpful in the home during the week, both for family devotions and in private prayer.

This particular selection has also been made in the hope that it will enrich the corporate prayer life of the congregation on Sunday. Some of the prayers may be helpful for private use in preparation for the service of worship. Many of the prayers are suitable for congregational use, the leader of worship and the people praying them together in unison. As a general rule, only one prayer for unison reading should be used in any one service of worship.

Some are prayers of adoration, others are prayers of confession, thanksgiving, and intercession, or prayers for illumination. The title of each prayer will suggest the appropriate place in the order of service where it could be used as the spoken prayer of the whole congregation. Other prayers are acts of commitment or dedication and may be used in place of a Scripture sentence in Word of Mission, or just before the Blessing.

A footnote at the conclusion of all these prayers identifies the person and the period to which the prayer is attributed. Some of the people who have written these prayers are listed in 'Other Commemorations'. The footnotes have been included in this section to remind us of the servants of Christ and people of prayer in ages past, and to give a sense of the timelessness of the great prayers of christian devotion.

VII   Selections from The Psalter

These Psalm portions are those provided in *Common Lectionary*, the three-year cycle of Scripture readings for Sundays and other principal days, which is currently in use in the Uniting Church.

This selection is from the complete Psalter of *The Book of Common Prayer, 1979*, of the Episcopal Church in the United States of America. This translation is also used by other churches in North America and has been acclaimed for its textual accuracy of translation from the original Hebrew, its beauty of literary style and its accommodation of inclusive language wherever possible. The kindness of the Episcopal Church in allowing this selection from its Psalter to be included in *Uniting in Worship* is warmly appreciated.

If a psalm reading is very short, it may be more effective for the leader of worship and the congregation to read all verses together in unison. However, the recommended way of reading the psalms is for the minister or leader of worship to read the first part of the verse and the congregation to read the second part. This maintains the parallelism of thought contained in each verse which is a literary characteristic of the Hebrew psalms. If this method is followed, the leader reads those parts in standard type and the congregation reads those parts in bold type. The response lines, in bold type, are also indented to help them stand out from the rest of the text.

The canticles, litanies and psalms in these resources for worship are set out for responsive reading. This responsive method may be used in the following ways:

(a) The minister or leader of worship reads the lines in standard type and the whole congregation reads the lines in bold type;

(b) The minister or leader of worship, together with the members of the choir, read the lines in standard type and the rest of the congregation reads the lines in bold type;

(c) The resource is read antiphonally between two parts of the congregation, normally those on the left side of the church and those on the right side. This is made more effective by a lector leading each part of the congregation.

It is an ancient practice in the church to say or sing a doxology in praise of the Trinity at the conclusion of the liturgical use of a psalm. There are some contemporary scholars who question this ancient practice, believing that readings from Old Testament Scriptures should be allowed to stand in their own right.

Some congregations may decide to always use a trinitarian doxology after a psalm, and other congregations may decide to omit it on all occasions. Another alternative is to vary the inclusion or exclusion of a doxology from week to week. If the predominant theme of the psalm is adoration or thanksgiving, it may seem appropriate to conclude with a christian doxology. If the psalm is predominantly confessional or intercessory, a few moments of silence after the psalm reading may be more helpful.

The posture of the congregation for the psalm reading should also be considered. As a general rule, if a sung doxology seems appropriate at the conclusion, the congregation should stand for the whole of the psalm reading, the music of the psalm tone being played after the psalm number is announced as the indication to the congregation to stand. If it seems more appropriate for the psalm to be followed by a few moments of silent reflection, the congregation should remain seated for the psalm reading.

The words of 'Glory to the Father' are set out in Canticle 13. Included also are 4 double and 2 single psalm tones. Providing the psalm tone is played after the psalm number is introduced and before the psalm is read, the selection of particular tones may vary from week to week or from season to season.

The Creeds of the Church

1 The Apostles' Creed

I believe in God, the Father almighty,
    creator of heaven and earth.

I believe in Jesus Christ, God's only Son, our Lord,
    who was conceived by the Holy Spirit,
    born of the Virgin Mary,
    suffered under Pontius Pilate,
    was crucified, died, and was buried;
    he descended to the dead.
    On the third day he rose again;
    he ascended into heaven,
    he is seated at the right hand of the Father,
    and he will come to judge the living and the dead.

I believe in the Holy Spirit,
    the holy catholic Church,
    the communion of saints,
    the forgiveness of sins,
    the resurrection of the body,
    and the life everlasting. Amen.

English Language Liturgical Consultation, 1987

2 The Nicene Creed

We believe in one God,
    the Father, the Almighty,
    maker of heaven and earth,
    of all that is, seen and unseen.

We believe in one Lord, Jesus Christ,
   the only Son of God,
   eternally begotten of the Father,
   God from God, Light from Light,
   true God from true God,
   begotten, not made,
   of one Being with the Father;
   through him all things were made.
For us and for our salvation
   he came down from heaven,
   was incarnate by the Holy Spirit of the Virgin Mary
   and became truly human.
   For our sake he was crucified under Pontius Pilate;
   he suffered death and was buried.
   On the third day he rose again
   in accordance with the Scriptures;
   he ascended into heaven
   and is seated at the right hand of the Father.
   He will come again in glory to judge the living and the dead,
   and his kingdom will have no end.

We believe in the Holy Spirit, the Lord, the giver of life,
   who proceeds from the Father,
   who with the Father and the Son is worshipped and glorified,
   who has spoken through the prophets.
   We believe in one holy catholic and apostolic Church.
   We acknowledge one baptism for the forgiveness of sins.
   We look for the resurrection of the dead,
   and the life of the world to come. Amen.

English Language Liturgical Consultation, 1987 alt.

Statements of Faith

1 The Beatitudes

Blessed are the poor in spirit,
  for theirs is the kingdom of heaven.

Blessed are those who mourn,
  for they shall be comforted.

Blessed are the gentle,
  for they shall inherit the earth.

Blessed are those who hunger and thirst for what is right,
  for they shall be satisfied.

Blessed are the merciful,
  for mercy shall be shown to them.

Blessed are the pure in heart,
  for they shall see God.

Blessed are the peacemakers,
  for they shall be called children of God.

Blessed are those who are persecuted in the cause of right,
  for theirs is the kingdom of heaven.

Blessed are you when others revile you and persecute you,
  and utter all kinds of evil against you falsely for my sake.

Rejoice and be glad,
  for your reward is great in heaven.

Matthew 5:3-12

2 The Incarnate Word

In the beginning was the Word,
and the Word was with God, and the Word was God.

He was in the beginning with God;
all things were made through him,
and without him was not anything made that was made.

In him was life,
and the life was the light of the world.

The light shines in the darkness,
and the darkness has not overcome it.

The true light that enlightens every one
was coming into the world.
He was in the world,
and the world was made through him,
yet the world knew him not.

He came to his own home,
and his own people received him not.

But to all who received him,
who believed in his name,
he gave power to become children of God;
who were born, not of blood,
nor of the will of the flesh,
nor of the will of man,
but of God.

And the Word became flesh and dwelt among us,
full of grace and truth;

we have beheld his glory,
glory as of the only Son from the Father.

And from his fullness have we all received,
  grace upon grace.

For the law was given through Moses;
  grace and truth came through Jesus Christ.

No one has ever seen God;
  the only Son, who is in the bosom of the Father,
  he has made him known.

John 1:1-5, 9-14, 16-18

3   The Image of the Invisible God

Jesus Christ is the image of the invisible God,
the firstborn of all creation;
in him all things in heaven and on earth were created,
things visible and invisible.

All things were created through him;
all were created for him.
He is before all else that is,
and in him everything continues in being.

Christ is the head of the body, the church;
he is the beginning,
the firstborn from the dead,
so that he may be first in everything.

For in him
all the fullness of God was pleased to dwell;
and Christ has reconciled to himself all things,
both on earth and in heaven,
making peace by the blood of his cross. Amen.

Colossians 1:15-20

4   Christ is Risen

Christ our Passover has been sacrificed for us;
therefore let us keep the feast,
not with the old leaven of corruption and wickedness,
but with the unleavened bread of sincerity and truth.
Alleluia!

Christ being raised from the dead will never die again;
death no longer has dominion over him.
The death that he died, he died to sin, once for all;
but the life he lives, he lives to God.
So also consider yourselves dead to sin,
and alive to God in Jesus Christ our Lord.
Alleluia!

Christ has been raised from the dead,
the firstfruits of those who have fallen asleep.
For since by a human being came death,
by a human being has come also the resurrection of the dead.
For as in Adam all die,
so also in Christ shall all be made alive.
Alleluia!

Adapted from:
1 Corinthians 5:7-8;
Romans 6:9-11;
1 Corinthians 15:20-22

5 Jesus Christ is Lord

We believe in Christ Jesus,
who, though he was in the form of God,
did not count equality with God
a thing to be grasped,
but emptied himself,
taking the form of a servant,
being born in human likeness.
And being found in human form he humbled himself
and became obedient to death,
even death on a cross.

Therefore God has highly exalted him
and bestowed on him the name which is above every name,
that at the name of Jesus every knee should bow,
in heaven and on earth and under the earth,
and every tongue confess to the glory of God:
Jesus Christ is Lord! Amen.

Philippians 2:5-11

6 The Gospel by which We are Saved

This is the gospel which we have received,
in which we stand,
and by which we are saved,
if we hold it fast:

that Christ died for our sins
according to the Scriptures,
that he was buried,
that he was raised on the third day,
and that he appeared first to the women,
then to Peter and to the Twelve,
and then to many faithful witnesses.

We believe that Jesus is the Christ,
the Son of the living God.
Jesus Christ is the first and the last,
the beginning and the end;
he is our Lord and our God. Amen.

1 Corinthians 15:1-6
Mark 16:1-9
Matthew 16:16
Revelation 22:13
John 20:28

7 God Works for Good in Everything

We believe that there is no condemnation
for those who are in Christ Jesus;
and we know that in everything God works for good
with those who love him,
who are called according to his purpose.

Leader
Who shall separate us from the love of Christ?
Shall tribulation or distress?
or persecution or famine?
or nakedness or peril or sword?

No, in all these things we are more than conquerors
through him who loved us.
For we are sure that neither death, nor life,
nor angels, nor principalities,
nor things present, nor things to come,
nor powers, nor height, nor depth,
nor anything else in all creation
will be able to separate us from the love of God
in Christ Jesus our Lord. Amen.

Romans 8:1, 28, 35, 37-39

8   We are a Pilgrim People

We believe in one God,
the Father, the Son, and the Holy Spirit.

We proclaim Jesus Christ, the crucified and risen One,
confessing him as Lord
to the glory of God the Father.

In the fellowship of the Holy Spirit,
we acclaim Jesus as the Lord of the church,
the Head over all things,
the beginning of a new creation.

We acknowledge that we live and work
between the time of Christ's death and resurrection
and the final consummation of all things
which he will bring.
We are a pilgrim people,
always on the way towards a promised goal;
on the way Christ feeds us with word and sacraments,
and we have the gift of the Spirit
in order that we may not lose the way.

We will live and work within the faith and unity
of the one holy catholic and apostolic Church,
bearing witness to that unity
which is both Christ's gift and his will.

We affirm that every member of the church
is engaged to confess the faith of Christ crucified.
Together with all the people of God,
we will serve the world for which Christ died.
And we await with hope the day of the Lord Jesus.

*Adapted from the Basis of Union
of the Uniting Church in Australia.*

9   God is with Us

We are not alone; we live in God's world.

We believe in God:
   who has created and is creating;
   who has come in Jesus, the Word made flesh,
    to reconcile and make new;
   who works in us and others by the Spirit.
We trust in God.

We are called to be the Church:
   to celebrate God's presence;
   to love and serve others;
   to seek justice and resist evil;
   to proclaim Jesus, crucified and risen,
      our judge and our hope.

In life, in death, in life beyond death,
   God is with us.
   We are not alone.
   Thanks be to God.

The United Church of Canada

10   The One Ministry of Christ

There are diverse gifts:
   but it is the same Spirit who gives them.

There are different ways of serving God:
   but it is the same Lord who is served.

God works through people in different ways:
   **but it is the same God
   whose purpose is achieved through them all.**

Each one of us is given a gift by the Spirit:
   and there is no gift without its corresponding service.

There is one ministry of Christ:
  and in this ministry we all share.

Together we are the body of Christ:
  and individually members of it.

Based on 1 Corinthians 12:4ff.
and Basis of Union, para. 13

11 Your Kingdom Come

Social Justice Affirmation

We believe in God,
    creator of the world and of all people;
and in Jesus Christ,
    incarnate among us, who died and rose again;
and in the Holy Spirit,
    present with us to guide, strengthen, and comfort.

We believe.
Lord, help our unbelief.

We rejoice in every sign of God's kingdom:
    in the upholding of human dignity and community;
    in every expression of love, justice, and reconciliation;
    in each act of self-giving on behalf of others;
    in the abundance of God's gifts
        entrusted to us that all may have enough;
    in all responsible use of the earth's resources.

Glory to God in the highest,
and peace to God's people on earth.

We confess our sin, individual and collective,
    by silence or action:
  through the violation of human dignity
    based on race, class, age, sex, nation, or faith;
  through the exploitation of people
    by greed and indifference;
  through the misuse of power
    in personal, communal, national, and international life;
  through the search for security
    by military and economic forces
    that threaten human existence:
  through the abuse of technology
    which endangers the earth and all life upon it.

Lord, have mercy.
Christ, have mercy.
Lord, have mercy.

We commit ourselves individually and as a community
    to the way of Christ;
  to take up the cross;
  to seek abundant life for all humanity;
  to struggle for peace with justice and freedom;
  to risk ourselves in faith, hope, and love,
    praying that God's kingdom may come.

For the kingdom, the power,
and the glory are yours,
now and for ever. Amen.

15th World Methodist Council,
Nairobi, Kenya, 1986

Canticles

1 Song of Peace

It shall come to pass in the latter days
that the mountain of the house of the Lord
shall be established as the highest of the mountains,
  and shall be raised above the hills.

And all the nations shall flow to it,
  and many peoples shall come, and say:
Come, let us go up to the mountain of the Lord,
  to the house of the God of Jacob:

That he may teach us his ways
  and that we may walk in his paths.
For out of Zion shall go forth the law,
  and the word of the Lord from Jerusalem.

God shall judge between the nations,
  and shall decide for many peoples:
and they shall beat their swords into ploughshares,
  and their spears into pruning hooks.

Nation shall not lift up sword against nation,
  neither shall they learn war any more.
O house of Jacob, come,
  let us walk in the light of the Lord.

Isaiah 2:2-5

2 The Lord's Servant

He was despised; he was rejected,
  a man of sorrows and acquainted with grief;
as one from whom people hide their faces,
  he was despised, and we esteemed him not.

Surely he has borne our griefs
  and carried our sorrows;
yet we esteemed him stricken,
  smitten by God and afflicted.

But he was wounded for our transgressions,
  he was bruised for our iniquities;
upon him was the punishment that made us whole,
  and with his stripes we are healed.

All we like sheep have gone astray;
  we have turned every one to his own way;
and the Lord has laid on him
  the iniquity of us all.

He was oppressed; he was afflicted,
  yet he opened not his mouth;
like a lamb that is lead to the slaughter,
  like a sheep that before its shearers is dumb,
  so he opened not his mouth.

And they made his grave with the wicked
  and with a rich man in his death,
although he had done no violence,
  and there was no deceit in his mouth.

He poured out his soul to death,
  and was numbered with the transgressors;
yet he bore the sins of many,
  and made intercession for the transgressors.

Isaiah 53:3-7, 9, 12b

3 Seek the Lord

Seek the Lord while he wills to be found;
   call upon God when he draws near.
Let the wicked forsake their ways
   and the evil ones their thoughts;
and let them turn to the Lord, who will have compassion,
   and to our God, who will richly pardon.

For my thoughts are not your thoughts,
   nor your ways my ways, says the Lord.
For as the heavens are higher than the earth,
so are my ways higher than your ways,
   and my thoughts than your thoughts.

For as rain and snow fall from the heavens
   and return not again, but water the earth,
bringing forth life and giving growth,
   seed for sowing and bread for eating,
so is my word which goes forth from my mouth;
   it will not return to me empty;
but it will accomplish that which I have purposed,
   and prosper in that for which I sent it.

Isaiah 55:6-11

4 The Glory of the Lord is Your Light

Arise, shine, for your light has come;
   the glory of the Lord has risen upon you.
Though night still covers the earth
   and darkness covers the nations,
over you will the Lord arise,
   over you will God's glory appear.
Nations will stream to your light,
   and kings to your dawning brightness.

At this sight you will grow radiant,
   your heart will thrill and rejoice;
for the riches of the sea will flow to you,
   the wealth of the nations will come to you.

They will bring gold and frankincense,
   singing the praise of the Lord.
They will come up, for acceptance, to my altar,
   to adorn the Temple of my glory.

Your gates will always be open;
   day or night, they will never be shut.
They will call you, The City of the Lord,
   The Zion of the Holy One of Israel.

Violence will no more be heard in your land,
   ruin or destruction within your borders;
you will name your walls, Salvation,
   you will call your gates, Praise.

No longer will the sun be your light by day,
   no longer the moon give you light by night;
the Lord will be your eternal light,
   your God will be your glory.

Isaiah 60:1-3, 5, 6b, 7b, 11a, 14b, 18, 19

5   Song from Ezekiel

I will take you from the nations,
and gather you from every country,
   and bring you home to your own land.

I will pour clean water upon you,
   purify you from all defilement,
   and cleanse you from all your idols.

A new heart I will give you,
  and put a new spirit within you;
I will take from your body the heart of stone,
  and give you a heart of flesh.

I will put my spirit within you,
  make you walk in my ways
  and observe my decrees.

You shall dwell in the land
I gave to your forebears;
  you shall be my people,
  and I will be your God.

Ezekiel 36:24-28

6   A Song of Creation

It is suggested that this song should be read antiphonally,
(indicated by **L** and **R**).

The two groups may be those on the left side and those on the
right side of the church. Alternatively, the leader of worship
and/or the choir may read antiphonally with the whole
congregation.

L   Glorify the Lord, all you works of the Lord,
    sing praise and highly exalt God for ever.
    In the firmament of God's power, glorify the Lord,
    sing praise and highly exalt God for ever.

R   Glorify the Lord, you angels and all powers of the Lord,
    O heavens and all waters above the heavens.
    Sun and moon and stars of the sky, glorify the Lord,
    sing praise and highly exalt God for ever.

L   Glorify the Lord, every shower of rain and fall of dew,
all winds and fire and heat.
Winter and summer, glorify the Lord,
sing praise and highly exalt God for ever.

R   Glorify the Lord, O nights and days,
O shining light and enfolding dark.
Storm clouds and thunderbolts, glorify the Lord,
sing praise and highly exalt God for ever.

L   Let the earth glorify the Lord.
Glorify the Lord, O mountains and hills,
and all that grows upon the earth,
sing praise and highly exalt God for ever.

R   Glorify the Lord, O springs of water, seas and streams,
O whales and all that move in the waters.
All birds of the air, glorify the Lord,
sing praise and highly exalt God for ever.

L   Glorify the Lord, O beasts of the wild,
and all you flocks and herds.
O men and women everywhere, glorify the Lord,
sing praise and highly exalt God for ever.

R   Let the people of God glorify the Lord,
sing praise and highly exalt God for ever.
Glorify the Lord, O priests and servants of the Lord,
sing praise and highly exalt God for ever.

All   Let us glorify the Lord: Father, Son, and Holy Spirit;
sing praise and highly exalt God for ever.
In the firmament of God's power, glorify the Lord,
sing praise and highly exalt God for ever.

Song of the Three Young Men, 35-48, 51-60

7 In Praise of Those who Have Died

Let us now sing the praises of the famous,
  our ancestors in their successive generations,
through whom the Lord established his renown,
  and revealed his majesty from the beginning.

Some were rulers over kingdoms,
  and were renowned for their strength.
Others were wise counsellors,
  who spoke out with prophetic power.
Others directed the people by their advice
and by their knowledge of the nation's law;
  out of their fund of wisdom they gave instruction.
Others were composers of music
  or writers of poetry.
Others were endowed with wealth and strength,
  living peacefully in their homes.

All these were honoured in their day,
  and were the glory of their times.
Some of these have left a name behind them,
  to be commemorated in history.

But there are others who are unremembered;
  they are dead; it is as though they had not existed,
they are now as though they had never been born,
  and so too, their children after them.

Not so our forebears; they were faithful people
  whose good deeds have never been forgotten.
Their prosperity is handed on to their descendants,
  and their inheritance to future generations.

Their children stand within the covenants,
  and, thanks to them, so do their children's children.
Their line will endure for all time,
  and their fame will never be blotted out.

Their bodies have been buried in peace,
   but their names live on for all generations.
Nations will proclaim their wisdom,
   and God's people will sing their praises.

Paraphrase of Ecclesiasticus 44:1-16

8   The Souls of the Righteous

The souls of the righteous are in the hand of God;
   no torment shall ever touch them.

In the eyes of the unwise they seemed to be dead,
   their departure was taken for defeat,
their going from us to be disaster;
   but they are in peace.

Though they appeared to be punished,
   their hope is rich in immortality.
Small their affliction, great their blessing;
   God proved and found them worthy of himself.

Like gold in a furnace he tried them,
   and accepted them as an oblation.

In the moment of God's coming
they shall kindle into flame,
   and run like sparks through the stubble.
They shall govern nations and peoples,
   and the Lord shall be their ruler for ever.

Wisdom 3:1-8

9   The Song of Mary

Magnificat

My soul proclaims the greatness of the Lord,
   my spirit rejoices in God my Saviour,
   for you, Lord, have looked with favour
      on your lowly servant.

From this day all generations will call me blessed:
   you, the Almighty, have done great things for me
   and holy is your name.

You have mercy on those who fear you,
   from generation to generation.

You have shown strength with your arm
   and scattered the proud in their conceit,

casting down the mighty from their thrones
   and lifting up the lowly.

You have filled the hungry with good things
   and sent the rich away empty.

You have come to the aid of your servant Israel,
   to remember the promise of mercy,

the promise made to our forebears,
   to Abraham and his children for ever.

Luke 1:46-55

10   The Song of Zechariah

Benedictus

Blessed are you, Lord, the God of Israel,
  you have come to your people and set them free.
You have raised up for us a mighty Saviour,
  born of the house of your servant David.

Through your holy prophets, you promised of old
to save us from our enemies,
  from the hands of all who hate us,
to show mercy to our forebears,
  and to remember your holy covenant.

This was the oath you swore to our father Abraham:
to set us free from the hands of our enemies,
  free to worship you without fear,
holy and righteous before you,
  all the days of our life.

And you, child, shall be called the prophet
of the Most High,
  for you will go before the Lord to prepare the way,
to give God's people knowledge of salvation
  by the forgiveness of their sins.

In the tender compassion of our God
  the dawn from on high shall break upon us,
to shine on those who dwell in darkness
and the shadow of death,
  and to guide our feet into the way of peace.

Luke 1:68-79

11 The Song of Simeon

Nunc Dimittis

Now, Lord, you let your servant go in peace:
your word has been fulfilled.

My own eyes have seen the salvation
which you have prepared in the sight of every people:

a light to reveal you to the nations
and the glory of your people Israel.

Luke 2:29-32

12 Great and Wonderful

Great and wonderful are your deeds, Lord God the Almighty.
Just and true are your ways, O Ruler of the nations.

Who shall not revere and praise your name, O Lord?
For you alone are holy.

All nations shall come and worship in your presence;
for your just dealings have been revealed.

To God who sits upon the throne and to the Lamb
be praise and honour, glory and might,
for ever and ever. Amen.

Revelation 15:3, 4

13 Glory to the Father

Gloria Patri

Glory to the Father,
and to the Son,
and to the Holy Spirit:
as it was in the beginning,
is now,
and will be for ever. Amen.

Pointed form:

Glory to the Father and / to the / Son //
and / to the / Holy / Spirit //
as it was in the be- / ginning • is / now //
and will / be for / ever • A- / men //

A

H. Smart

B

R. Cooke

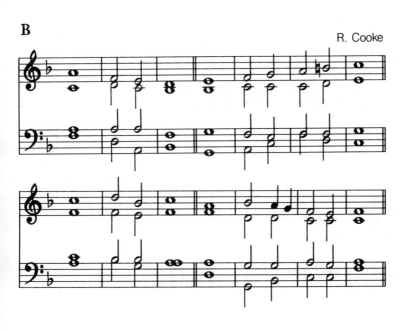

C

R. Farrant

Pointed form:

Glory to the Father and / to the / Son //
and / to the / Holy / Spirit //
as it was in the be- / ginning • is / now //
and will / be for / ever • A- / men //

D

Adapted from Luther

Descant

E

J. Turle

F

G. J. Elvey

14 Glory to God in the Highest

Gloria in Excelsis

Glory to God in the highest,
and peace to God's people on earth.

Lord God, heavenly King,
almighty God and Father,
we worship you, we give you thanks,
we praise you for your glory.

Lord Jesus Christ, only Son of the Father,
Lord God, Lamb of God,
you take away the sin of the world:
have mercy on us;
you are seated at the right hand of the Father:
receive our prayer.

For you alone are the Holy One,
you alone are the Lord,
you alone are the Most High,
Jesus Christ,
with the Holy Spirit,
in the glory of God the Father. Amen.

15 Lamb of God

Agnus Dei

Jesus, Lamb of God,
have mercy on us.

Jesus, bearer of our sins,
have mercy on us.

Jesus, redeemer of the world,
grant us peace.

Lamb of God, you take away the sin of the world,
have mercy on us.

Lamb of God, you take away the sin of the world,
have mercy on us.

Lamb of God, you take away the sin of the world,
grant us peace.

16   Saviour of the World

Salvator Mundi

Jesus, Saviour of the world,
come to us in your mercy;
we look to you to save and help us.

By your cross and your life laid down
you set your people free;
we look to you to save and help us.

When they were about to perish
you saved your disciples;
we look to you to come to our help.

In the greatness of your mercy,
loose us from our chains;
forgive the sins of all your people.

Make yourself known as our Saviour
and mighty Deliverer;
save and help us that we may praise you.

Come now and dwell with us,
Lord Christ Jesus;
hear our prayer and be with us always.

And when you come in your glory,
  make us to be one with you
  and to share the life of your kingdom.

17   We Praise You, O God

Te Deum Laudamus

Part 1

We praise you, O God,
  we acclaim you as Lord;
all creation worships you,
  the Father everlasting.

To you all angels, all the powers of heaven,
  the cherubim and seraphim, sing in endless praise:
Holy, holy, holy Lord, God of power and might,
  heaven and earth are full of your glory.

The glorious company of apostles praise you.
The noble fellowship of prophets praise you.
  The white-robed army of martyrs praise you.

Throughout the world the holy Church acclaims you:
  Father, of majesty unbounded,
your true and only Son, worthy of all praise,
  the Holy Spirit, advocate and guide.

Part 2

You, Christ, are the king of glory,
  the eternal Son of the Father.

When you took our flesh to set us free
  you humbly chose the Virgin's womb.

You overcame the sting of death
  and opened the kingdom of heaven to all believers.

You are seated at God's right hand in glory.
We believe that you will come to be our judge.

Come then, Lord, and help your people,
bought with the price of your own blood,
and bring us with your saints
to glory everlasting.

Versicles and Responses after the Te Deum Laudamus

Save your people, Lord, and bless your inheritance.
Govern and uphold them now and always.

Day by day we bless you.
We praise your name for ever.

Keep us today, Lord, from all sin.
Have mercy on us, Lord, have mercy.

Lord, show us your love and mercy,
for we have put our trust in you.

In you, Lord, is our hope:
let us never be put to shame.

18   A Canticle for Advent

Blessed are you, O Lord our God,
ruler of the universe,
creator of light and life.

Restore us, O Lord God of hosts;
show us the light of your countenance,
 and we shall be saved.

Will you not give us life again,
that your people may rejoice in you?

Show us your mercy, O Lord,
  and grant us your salvation.

In this holy season
you renew your covenant promise:
  to reveal among us the splendour of your glory,
  enfleshed and visible in Jesus Christ your Son.

Through the prophets
you teach us to hope for his reign of peace.
  Through the outpouring of the Spirit
  you open our blindness to the glory of your presence.

Strengthen us in our weakness.
  Support us in our stumbling efforts to do your will,
  and free our tongues to sing your praise.

Blessed is the King who comes in the name of the Lord!
  Peace in heaven and glory in the highest.

19   A Canticle for Christmas and Epiphany

Blessed are you, O Christ, our God;
  you were before time began,
  and came into the world to save us.

Blessed are you, Sun of righteousness;
  you shine with the Father's love
  and illumine the whole universe.

Blessed are you, Son of Mary;
  born a child,
  you shared our humanity.

Blessed are you, Son of David;
  born to rule,
  you received gifts from the wise men.

Blessed are you, Son of Man;
  baptised by John,
  you saved us from ourselves.

Blessed are you, heavenly King;
  teaching and preaching, healing and comforting,
  you proclaimed the kingdom.

With all the voices of heaven
we celebrate the coming of our Saviour.
  Let heaven and earth shout their praise.

With all the creatures on earth
we sing and dance at your birth.
  Praise and glory to you, O Lord Jesus Christ.

20   A Canticle for Lent

Blessed are you, O Lord our God,
  the Leader of your people Israel.

You gave them a pillar of cloud by day,
  and a pillar of fire by night.

During these forty days
you lead us into the desert of repentance,
  that in this pilgrimage of prayer
  we may learn to be your people once more.

You call us to turn away from our sins
in the far country of our selfish living;
  and welcoming us home again,
  you take us to your heart.

You lead us along the road of discipleship;
  and mark us with the sign of the cross.

Be with us in these journey days;
  for without your light we shall lose the way.

To you, our God, be dominion and glory,
  now and through the ages of ages.

21 A Canticle for Easter

Exsultet

Rejoice, heavenly powers! Sing, choirs of angels!
Exult, all creation around God's throne!
  Jesus Christ, our King, is risen!
  Sound the trumpet of salvation!

Rejoice, O earth, in shining splendour,
radiant in the brightness of your King!
  Christ has conquered! Glory fills you!
  Darkness vanishes for ever!

Rejoice, O holy church! Exult in glory!
The risen Saviour shines upon you!
  Let this place resound with joy,
  echoing the mighty song of all God's people.

It is truly right
that with full hearts and minds and voices
  we should praise the unseen God, the all-powerful Father,
  and his only Son, our Lord Jesus Christ.

This is our passover feast,
when Christ, the true Lamb, is slain,
  whose blood consecrates the homes of all believers.

This is the day when christians everywhere,
washed clean of sin and freed from all defilement,
  are restored to grace and grow together in holiness.

This is the day when Jesus Christ
broke the chains of death,
   and rose triumphant from the grave.

Father, how wonderful your care for us!
How boundless your merciful love!
   To ransom slaves, you gave away your Son!

Day truly blessed,
when heaven is wedded to earth,
   and we are reconciled to God!

Therefore, heavenly Father,
in the joy of this day,
   receive our sacrifice of praise,
   your church's solemn offering.

(Accept this Easter candle.
   May Christ dispel the darkness of our night!)

May the Morning Star which never sets
find the flame of our love always burning.
   May Christ, that Morning Star,
      who came back from the dead,
   shed his peaceful light on all the world.

Adapted from the Liturgy of the Easter Vigil,
Roman Catholic Church

22   A Canticle for Pentecost

Holy is God!
   Holy the mighty One!
Holy the immortal One!
   Holy God, have mercy on us.

Blessed are you, most high God!
When you came down at Babel,
you confused the tongues and divided the nations.
**But when you distributed the tongues of fire at Pentecost,
you called all people to unity.
Therefore, with one accord,
we glorify the Holy Spirit.**

Blessed are you, most high God!
When you sent the Spirit upon the apostles,
the Hebrews were struck with awe;
they heard them speak in many tongues,
as the Spirit inspired them.
**They knew them to be illiterate,
and now they saw them wise;
speaking divine truths
and bringing Gentiles to believe.**

When the faithless ones
witnessed the power of the Spirit,
they took it to be drunkenness
when in fact it was salvation for the faithful.
**Therefore, with one accord,
we glorify the Holy Spirit.**

Holy God, Lover of souls,
make us worthy of the revelation of this Spirit
within us.
**Holy Spirit, the Spirit of truth,
present in all places and filling all things,
the giver of life and the treasury of blessings,
come and dwell in us.**

You, Holy Spirit, provide every gift:
you renew the church and restore wholeness;
you shed abroad the love of God;

you grant wisdom to the illiterate;
you use simple fishermen
through whom you begin to draw the whole world
into Christ's net.

Through you we have seen the true light,
we have received the spiritual gifts,
we have found the true faith.
Therefore, O Counsellor,
equal in majesty with the Father and the Son,
glory to you, Lord.

Holy the immortal One,
the Spirit, the Comforter,
who proceeds from the Father and reposes in the Son.
All holy Trinity,
glory to you.

Adapted from the Liturgy of the Orthodox Church

23   In Praise of the Trinity

Worthy of praise from every mouth,
worthy of confession from every tongue,

worthy of worship from every creature,
is your glorious name, O Father, Son, and Holy Spirit.

For you created the world in your grace,
and by your compassion you saved the world.

To your majesty, O God,
ten thousand times ten thousand bow down and adore,
singing and praising without ceasing, and saying:

Holy, holy, holy, Lord God of hosts;
heaven and earth are full of your praises.
Hosanna in the highest.

Nestorian Liturgy, 5th century

24   O Gracious Light

Phos Hilaron

O gracious Light,
pure brightness of the everliving Father in heaven,
   O Jesus Christ, holy and blessed!

Now as we come to the setting of the sun,
and our eyes behold the vesper light,
   we sing your praises, O God:
   Father, Son and Holy Spirit.

You are worthy at all times
to be praised by happy voices,
   O Son of God, O Giver of life,
   and to be glorified through all the worlds.

25   An Evening Canticle

Blessed are you, O Lord, our God,
ruler of the universe!
   Your word brings on the dusk of evening,
   your wisdom creates both day and night.

You led your people Israel by a pillar of cloud by day
   and a pillar of fire by night.

Enlighten our darkness by the light of your Christ.
   May his word be a lamp to our feet
   and a light to our path.

For you are full of loving kindness
for your whole creation;
  and we, your creatures, glorify you,
  Father, Son, and Holy Spirit.

Living and eternal God, rule over us always.
  Blessed be the Lord, whose word makes evening fall.

26   Versicles and Responses

Open our lips, O Lord:
And we shall declare your praise.

O God, make speed to save us.
O Lord, make haste to help us.

Glory to the Father,
and to the Son,
and to the Holy Spirit:
as it was in the beginning,
is now,
and will be for ever. Amen

Let us praise the Lord.
The Lord's name be praised.

Open our lips, O Lord; And we shall de-clare your praise.

O God, make speed to save us. O Lord, make haste to help us.

Glory to the Father, As it was in the beginning, A - men.
and to the Son, is now, and will be for/ever
and to the Holy Spirit:

Let us praise the Lord. The Lord's name be praised.

27   The Australian National Anthem

Australians all, let us rejoice,
for we are young and free;
we've golden soil and wealth for toil,
our home is girt by sea.
Our land abounds in nature's gifts
of beauty rich and rare;
in history's page, let every stage
advance Australia fair.

In joyful strains then let us sing:
Advance, Australia fair!

Another verse alt.

Beneath the radiant Southern Cross
we'll toil with heart and hand,
to make this Commonwealth of ours
a just and righteous land.
For those who've come across the seas
we've boundless plains to share;
with courage let us all combine
to advance Australia fair.

In joyful strains then let us sing:
Advance, Australia fair!

Litanies

1　The Great Litany

I　Prayer of approach to God

Let us pray:

God the Father,
have mercy on us.

God the Son,
have mercy on us.

God the Holy Spirit,
have mercy on us.

Holy, blessed, and glorious Trinity,
have mercy on us.

II　Prayers for deliverance

From all evil and mischief;
from pride, vanity, and hypocrisy;
from envy, hatred, and malice;
and from every evil intent;
Good Lord, deliver us.

From laziness, worldliness, and love of money;
from hardness of heart,
and contempt for your word and your laws;
Good Lord, deliver us.

From sins of body and mind;
from the deceits of the world, the flesh, and the devil;
Good Lord, deliver us.

From famine and disaster;
from violence, murder, and dying unprepared;
Good Lord, deliver us.

In all times of sorrow;
in all times of joy;
in the hour of death;
and at the day of judgment;
  Good Lord, deliver us.

By the mystery of your holy incarnation;
by your birth, childhood, and obedience;
by your baptism, fasting, and temptation;
  Good Lord, deliver us.

By your ministry in word and work;
by your mighty acts of power;
and by your preaching of the kingdom;
  Good Lord, deliver us.

By your agony and trial;
by your cross and passion;
and by your precious death and burial;
  Good Lord, deliver us.

By your mighty resurrection;
by your glorious ascension;
and by your sending of the Holy Spirit;
  Good Lord, deliver us.

IV Prayers for the church

Hear our prayers, O Lord our God.
  Hear us, good Lord.

Govern and direct your holy church;
fill it with love and truth;
and grant it that unity which is your will.
  Hear us, good Lord.

Give us boldness to preach the gospel in all the world,
and to make disciples of all nations.
Hear us, good Lord.

Enlighten your ministers with knowledge and understanding,
that, by their teaching and their lives,
they may proclaim your word.
Hear us, good Lord.

Give your people grace to hear and receive your word,
and to bring forth the fruit of the Spirit.
Hear us, good Lord.

Bring into the way of truth
all who have erred and are deceived.
Hear us, good Lord.

Strengthen those who stand;
comfort and help the faint-hearted;
raise up the fallen;
and finally beat down Satan under our feet.
Hear us, good Lord.

V   Prayers for the world and for our own country

Guide the leaders of the nations
into the ways of peace and justice.
Hear us, good Lord.

Strengthen your servant Elizabeth our queen,
that she may put her trust in you,
and seek your honour and glory.
Hear us, good Lord.

Inspire and direct all members of parliament,
both of our Commonwealth and of this State,
and grant them wisdom and understanding.
Hear us, good Lord.

Bless those who administer our law,
that they may uphold justice, honesty, and truth.
Hear us, good Lord.

Teach us to use the resources of the earth to your glory,
and for the good of all people.
Hear us, good Lord.

Bless and keep all your people.
Hear us, good Lord.

VI Prayers for all people

Help and comfort the lonely,
the bereaved, and the oppressed.
Lord, have mercy.

Keep in safety those who travel,
and all who are in danger.
Lord, have mercy.

Heal the sick in body and mind,
and provide for the homeless, the hungry, and the destitute.
Lord, have mercy.

Show your pity on prisoners and refugees,
and all who are in trouble.
Lord, have mercy.

Forgive our enemies, persecutors, and slanderers,
and turn their hearts.
Lord, have mercy.

Hear us as we remember those who have died
in the peace of Christ:
those who have confessed the faith before the world,
those whom we remember,
and those whose faith is known to you alone;
and grant us with them a share in your eternal kingdom.
Lord, have mercy.

Give us true repentance;
forgive us our sins of negligence and ignorance,
and our deliberate sins;
and grant us the grace of the Holy Spirit
to amend our lives according to your holy word.
  Holy God,
  holy and mighty, holy and immortal One,
  have mercy on us.

Alternative Service Book, 1980,
Church of England (adapted)

2   A Litany of Invocation

Come to us, God of peace.
Come with your healing and your reconciling power.
Come, that fear may be cast out by love;
that weapons may be replaced by trust;
that violence may give way to gentleness:
  Come to us, God of peace.

Come to us, God of justice.
Come with your righteous judgments and your mercy.
Come, that we may hear the cries of the oppressed
    in every land;
that we may see the suffering of the poor in our own land;
that we may return to the way of righteousness
    and compassion:
  Come to us, God of justice.

Come to us, God of love.
Come with your extravagant kindness and your goodness.
Come, that we may see you in the people
    of every race and culture;
that we may embrace you in the lonely, the bereaved
    and the rejected;
that we may be an accepting and a caring church:
    Come to us, God of love.

Come to us, God of unity.
Come with your forgiveness and your healing grace.
Come, that we may witness to reconciliation
    for a divided world;
that we may gather around Christ's table as one people;
that we may affirm one church, one faith, one Lord:
    Come to us, God of unity.

Come to us, God of hope.
Come to us with your promises,
    come in your mysterious presence.
Come, that we may marvel at your faithfulness
    in past generations;
that we may celebrate the new things you are doing
    among us today;
that we may be your pilgrim people
    on our journey to your kingdom:
    Come to us, God of hope.

Adapted from a prayer in the Opening Service
of the Fourth Assembly, 1985,
Uniting Church in Australia

3 A Litany of Thanksgiving

Give thanks to the Lord, for he is good.
God's love is everlasting.

Come, let us praise God joyfully.
Let us come to God with thanksgiving.

For the good world;
for things great and small, beautiful and awesome;
for seen and unseen splendours:
Thank you, God.

For human life;
for talking and moving and thinking together;
for common hopes
and hardships shared from birth until dying:
Thank you, God.

For work to do and strength to work;
for the comradeship of labour;
for exchanges of good humour and encouragement:
Thank you, God.

For marriage;
for the mystery and joy of flesh made one;
for mutual forgiveness, and burdens shared;
for secrets kept in love:
Thank you, God.

For family;
for living together and eating together;
for family amusements and family pleasures:
Thank you, God.

For children;
for their energy and curiosity;
for their imagination and creativity;
for their startling frankness and their sudden sympathies:
Thank you, God.

For young people;
for their high hopes and visions for the future;
for their irreverence towards worn-out values;
for their search for freedom and their solemn vows:
Thank you, God.
For growing up and growing old;
for wisdom deepened by experience;
for rest in leisure;
and for time made precious by its passing:
Thank you, God.
For your help in times of doubt and sorrow;
for healing our diseases;
for preserving us in temptation and danger:
Thank you, God.
For the church into which we have been called;
for the good news we receive by word and sacrament;
for our life together in the Lord:
Thank you, God.
For the Holy Spirit,
who guides our steps
and brings us gifts of faith and love;
who prays in us and prompts our grateful worship:
We praise you, God our Father.
For your Son Jesus Christ,
who lived and died
and lives again for our salvation;
for our hope in him;
and for the joy of serving him:
We praise you, God our Father.
Give thanks to the Lord, for he is good.
God's love is everlasting. Amen.

The Worshipbook Services, 1970,
Presbyterian Church, U.S.A.
(adapted)

4 A Litany of General Intercession 1

O Lord our God,
you hear our prayers before we speak,
and answer before we know our need.
Although we cannot pray as we ought,
may your Spirit pray in us,
drawing us to you and towards our neighbours.
  Amen.

We pray for the whole creation:
may all things work together for good,
until, by your design,
your children inherit the earth and order it wisely.
  Let the whole creation praise you, Lord our God.

We pray for the church of Jesus Christ;
that, begun, maintained and promoted by the Holy Spirit,
it may be true, engaging, glad, and active,
doing your will.
  Let the church be always faithful, Lord our God.

We pray for peace in the world.
Disarm weapons, silence guns,
and put out ancient hate that smoulders still,
or flames in sudden conflict.
Create goodwill between every race and nation.
  Bring peace on earth, O God.

We pray for enemies, as Christ commanded;
for those who oppose us or scheme against us,
who are also children of your love.

May we be kept from infectious hate
or sick desire for vengeance.
Make friends of enemies, O God.

We pray for those involved in world government,
in agencies of control or compassion,
who work for the reconciling of the nations:
keep them hopeful, and work with them for peace.
Unite our broken world, O God.

We pray for those who govern us,
for those who make and administer our laws.
May this country always be a land of free people
who welcome exiles and work for justice.
Govern those who govern us, O God.

II   For those in need

We pray for those who are poor, those who are hungry,
in need of employment, homes or education.
Increase in us, and in all who prosper,
concern for the disinherited.
Care for the poor, O God.

We pray for social outcasts;
for those excluded by their own aggression
or by the harshness of others.
May we accept those whom our world names unacceptable,
and so show your mighty love.
Welcome the alienated, O God.

We pray for sick people who suffer pain,
or struggle with demons of the mind,
who silently cry out for healing:
may they be patient, brave, and trusting.
Heal the sick and troubled, O God.

We pray for the dying, who face the final mystery:
may they enjoy light and life intensely,
keep dignity, and greet death unafraid,
believing in your love.
   Have mercy on the dying, O God.

We pray for those whose tears are not yet dry,
who listen for familiar voices and look for familiar faces:
in their loss, may they affirm all that you promise in Jesus,
who prepares a place for us within your spacious love.
   Comfort those who mourn, O God.

We pray for people who are alone and lonely,
who have no one to call in easy friendship:
may they be remembered, befriended,
and know your care for them.
   Visit lonely people, O God.

We pray for people who do not believe,
who are shaken by doubt, or have turned against you.
Open their eyes to see beyond our broken fellowship
the wonders of your love displayed in Jesus of Nazareth,
and to follow when he calls them.
   Conquer doubt with faith, O God.

We pray for families, for parents and children:
may they enjoy each other, honour freedoms,
and forgive as freely as we are all forgiven
in your huge mercy.
   Keep families in love, O God.

We pray for young and old:
give impatient youth true vision,
and experienced age openness to new things.
Let both praise your name.
   Join youth and age together, O God.

We pray for people everywhere:
may they come into their own as children of God,
and inherit the kingdom prepared in Jesus Christ,
the Lord of all and Saviour of the world.
  Hear our prayers, almighty God,
  in the name of Jesus Christ,
  who prays with us and for us,
  to whom be praise for ever. Amen.

The Worshipbook Services, 1970,
Presbyterian Church, U.S.A. (adapted)

5 A Litany of General Intercession 2

With confidence and trust let us pray to the Lord,
saying: Lord, have mercy.

For the one holy catholic and apostolic Church
throughout the world,
we pray to you, Lord.
  Lord, have mercy.

For the mission of the church, that in faithful witness
it may preach the gospel to the ends of the earth,
we pray to you, Lord.
  Lord, have mercy.

For those preparing for baptism or confirmation,
and for their teachers, elders, and christian friends,
we pray to you, Lord.
  Lord, have mercy.

For peace in the world,
that a spirit of respect and reconciliation
may grow among nations and peoples,
we pray to you, Lord.
  Lord, have mercy.

For the poor, the persecuted, the sick, and all who suffer;
for refugees, prisoners, and all in danger;
that they may be relieved and protected,
we pray to you, Lord.
Lord, have mercy.

For all whom we have injured or offended,
we pray to you, Lord.
Lord, have mercy.

For grace to amend our lives
and to further the reign of God,
we pray to you, Lord.
Lord, have mercy.

Book of Alternative Services, 1985,
Anglican Church of Canada
(adapted)

6   A Litany for the Church

Almighty God,
you built your church on the rock of human faith and trust;
we praise you for Jesus Christ,
the foundation and cornerstone of all we believe.
We praise you, O God.

For the great people of history,
whose love for your church
made it a willing instrument of your care and mercy;
who placed you first in their lives
and held to their faith in good times and in bad:
We praise you, O God.

Save us, O God, from living in the past,
and from resting on the work and witness of others.
Let us catch a new vision and make a new beginning,
that we may faithfully serve you
in this congregation and in our world today.
  Lord, have mercy.

Keep us, O God, from lack of reverence for truth and beauty;
from artificial life and worship,
from all that is hollow or insincere.
  Lord, have mercy.

Spare us, O God, from pride that excludes others
from the shelter of your love;
from the selfishness that uses your church
as a means of getting social position or personal glory.
  Lord, have mercy.

Save us, O God, from sin and worldliness
which deny the saving power of the gospel;
from shallowness of faith and hypocrisy of life
which cause others to remain empty or be disillusioned.
  Lord, have mercy.

That we may accept the responsibility of our freedom,
the burden of our privilege;
and so conduct ourselves
that we may bring others to faith in Christ;
  O God, be our strength.

That we may not be content with a secondhand faith,
worshipping words rather than the Word;
but that we may find joy in study of the Bible,
and growth in exposure to new insights;
   O God, be our strength.

That we may be actively engaged in the life
of our congregation and parish,
our presbytery and community,
sharing in Christ's mission to the world,
and always seeking the common good;
   O God, be our strength.

That we may find in your church
a prod to our imaginations,
a shock to our laziness,
and a source of power to do your will;
   O God, be our strength.

O God,
you gave us minds to know you,
hearts to love you,
and voices to sing your praise.
Send the Holy Spirit among us,
that, confronted by your truth,
we may worship and serve you as we should;
through Jesus Christ our Lord.
   Amen.

*The Worshipbook Services, 1970
Presbyterian Church, U.S.A.
(adapted)*

7 A Litany for Christian Unity 1

I

O God,
you have welcomed us by baptism into one holy church,
and joined us by faith
to christian people in every time and place.
May your church on earth
be a sign of the communion you promise,
where we shall all be one with Christ,
and joyful in your kingdom.
  Amen.

From clinging to power that prevents christian unity;
from thinking that forms of government are perfect,
or councils of the church infallible:
  Good Lord, deliver us.

From mistaken zeal that will not compromise;
from religious pride that belittles the faith of others,
claiming true wisdom, but failing to love:
  Good Lord, deliver us.

From a worldly mind that drums up party spirit;
from divisiveness, and a refusal to listen to others;
from protecting systems that have had their day:
  Good Lord, deliver us.

II

As you sent disciples into every land, O God,
gather them now from the ends of the earth
into one fellowship
that chooses your purpose and praises your name,
in one faith, hope and love.
  Amen.

Make us one, Lord,
in our eagerness to speak the good news
and to set all captives free.
  Grant us the Holy Spirit.

Make us one, Lord,
in concern for the poor, the hurt, and the down-trodden,
to show them your love.
  Grant us the Holy Spirit.

Make us one, Lord,
in worship and fellowship, breaking bread together
and singing your praise with single voice.
  Grant us the Holy Spirit.

Make us one, Lord,
in faithfulness to Jesus Christ, who never fails us,
and who will come again in triumph.
  Grant us the Holy Spirit.

Grant us the Holy Spirit, God our Father,
so that we may have among us
the mind that was in Christ Jesus;
and proclaim him to the world.
May every knee bow down,
and every tongue confess him as Lord,
to the glory of your holy name.
  Amen.

The Worshipbook Services, 1970
Presbyterian Church, U.S.A.
(adapted)

8   A Litany for Christian Unity 2

Across all our barriers of language,
race, and nationality:
Unite us, Jesus.

Across all our mutual ignorance,
prejudice, and hostility:
Unite us, Jesus.

Across all our differences of thought,
outlook, and religious allegiance:
Unite us, Jesus.

O God, for your greater glory:
Gather together your separated people.

O God, for the triumph of goodness and truth:
Gather together your separated people.

O God, that there may be one flock
and one sheep fold:
Gather together your separated people.

O God, to confound the pride of Satan
and his assaults:
Gather together your separated people.

O God, that peace may reign in the world at last:
Gather together your separated people.

O God, for the greater joy of the heart of your Son:
Gather together your separated people.

> *A prayer of Fr Couturier of Lyons, France,*
> *who initiated the Week of Prayer for the unity*
> *of all christians. (adapted)*

Another way of praying this prayer is for the leader and people to say
alternate stanzas.

9 A Litany for World Peace

Remember, O Lord, the peoples of the world,
divided into many nations and tongues.
Deliver us from every evil
that gets in the way of your saving purpose;
and fulfil the promise of peace to your people on earth;
through Jesus Christ our Lord.
    Amen.

Silence

From the curse of war
and the human sin that causes war;
    O Lord, deliver us.

From pride that turns its back on you,
and from unbelief that will not call you Lord;
    O Lord, deliver us.

From national vanity that poses as patriotism;
from loud-mouthed boasting,
and blind self-worship that admits no guilt;
    O Lord, deliver us.

From the self-righteousness that will not compromise,
and from selfishness that gains by the oppression of others;
    O Lord, deliver us.

From the lust for money or power
that drives people to kill;
    O Lord, deliver us.

From trusting in the weapons of war,
and mistrusting the councils of peace;
    O Lord, deliver us.

From hearing and believing propaganda,
and speaking lies about other nations;
  O Lord, deliver us.

From groundless suspicions and fears
that stand in the way of reconciliation;
  O Lord, deliver us.

From words and deeds that encourage discord,
prejudice, and hatred;
from everything that prevents the human family
from fulfilling your promise of peace;
  O Lord, deliver us.

O God our Father,
we pray for all your children on earth,
of every nation and of every race;
  That they may be strong to do your will.

  Silence

We pray for the church in all the world;
  Give peace in our time, O Lord.

For the United Nations;
  Give peace in our time, O Lord.

For the leaders of the nations,
and for all politicians, ambassadors, and diplomats;
  Give peace in our time, O Lord.

For international federations of labour,
industry, and commerce;
  Give peace in our time, O Lord.

For worldwide agencies of compassion
which bind wounds and feed the hungry;
  Give peace in our time, O Lord.

For the World Council of Churches and its agencies;
  Give peace in our time, O Lord.

For all who, in any way,
work to further the cause of peace and goodwill;
  Give peace in our time, O Lord.

For ordinary people in many lands who live in peace,
and who long for peace for all people;
  Give peace in our time, O Lord.

Eternal God,
use us, despite our ignorance and weakness,
to help bring about your holy will.
Hasten the day when all people shall live together
in your love;
for the kingdom, the power, and the glory are yours
now and for ever.
  Amen.

10   Prayers of the People 1

It is appropriate for a lay person to lead these prayers.

The leader may add particular concerns to each bidding.

In the silence after each bidding, the people offer
their own prayers, either silently or aloud.

I ask your prayers for the church:
for the Uniting Church in Australia,
for N, president of the Assembly,

for N our moderator and N our chairperson of presbytery,
for all ministers and people,
and for this community of faith.
Pray for the holy catholic Church.

Silence

Almighty and everlasting God,
by your Spirit the whole body of your faithful people
is governed and sanctified.
Receive our supplications and prayers,
which we offer before you
for all members of your holy church,
that in our vocation and ministry
we may truly and devoutly serve you;
through our Lord and Saviour Jesus Christ.
   Amen.

I ask your prayers for peace,
for goodwill among nations,
and for the well-being of all people.

Silence

Almighty God,
kindle, we pray, in every heart the true love of peace,
and guide with your wisdom
those who take counsel for the nations of the earth,
that justice and peace may increase,
until the earth is filled with the knowledge of your love;
through Jesus Christ our Lord.
   Amen.

I ask your prayers for the poor, the sick, the hungry,
the oppressed, and those in prison.
Pray for those in any need or trouble.

Silence

Gracious God,
the comfort of all who sorrow,
the strength of all who suffer,
hear the cry of those in misery and need.
In their afflictions show them your mercy,
and give us, we pray, the strength to serve them,
for the sake of him who suffered for us,
your Son Jesus Christ our Lord.
    Amen.

I ask your prayers for the mission of the church.
Pray for the coming of God's kingdom
among all nations and peoples.

Silence

O Lord our God,
you have made all races and nations to be one family,
and you sent your Son Jesus Christ
to proclaim the good news of salvation to all people.
Pour out your Spirit on the whole creation,
bring the nations of the world into your fellowship,
and hasten the coming of your kingdom.
We ask this through the same Jesus Christ our Lord.
    Amen.

I ask your prayers of thanksgiving
for those who have died in the peace of Christ,
for those whom we remember,
and for those whose faith is known to God alone.
Pray that God may be glorified in all the saints.

Silence

O God, the giver of eternal life,
we give you thanks and praise
for the wonderful grace and virtue
declared in all your saints.
Grant to us, and to all who have died
in the hope of the resurrection,
a share in the victory of our Lord Jesus Christ
and fullness of joy in the fellowship of all your saints.
All this we ask in the name of Jesus Christ our Lord.
Amen.

Let us give thanks to almighty God for all his goodness.

Silence

You are worthy, O Lord our God,
to receive glory and honour and power.
You are worthy to receive blessing and praise,
now and for ever.
For yours is the majesty, O Father, Son, and Holy Spirit;
the kingdom, the power and the glory are yours,
now and for ever. Amen.

11   Prayers of the People 2

It is appropriate for a lay person to lead these prayers.

In peace, we pray to you, Lord God.

For all people in their daily life and work;
**for our families, friends, and neighbours,
and for those who are alone.**

For this community, our country, and the world;
for all who work for justice, freedom, and peace.

For the just and proper use of your creation;
for the victims of hunger, fear, injustice and oppression.

For all who are in danger, sorrow, or any kind of trouble;
**for those who minister to the sick,
the friendless and the needy.**

For the peace and unity of the Church of God;
**for all who proclaim the gospel,
and for all who seek the truth.**

For the Uniting Church in Australia,
for N, president of the Assembly,
for N our moderator and for N our chairperson of presbytery,
(for N our minister of the Word),
for our elders and members of the parish council,
and for all who hold office in this congregation;
for all who serve God in the church.

For our own needs,
and for others for whom you have called us to pray.

Silence

The people may offer their own petitions,
either silently or aloud.

Hear us, Lord;
for your mercy is great.

We thank you, Lord, for all the blessings of life.

Silence

The people may offer their own thanksgivings, either silently or aloud.

We will exalt you, O God our king;
and praise your name for ever and ever.

We give thanks for all those who have died
in the peace of Christ,
and for the promise of your eternal kingdom.

Silence

The people may offer their own thanksgivings, either silently or aloud.

In Christ you have called us to eternal glory;
to you be praise for ever and ever.

The collect of the day may be said.

The leader concludes with the following collect:

Gracious God,
you have heard the prayers of your faithful people;
you know our needs before we ask,
and our ignorance in asking.
Grant our requests as may be best for us.
This we ask in the name of your Son,
Jesus Christ our Lord.
Amen.

Book of Common Prayer, 1979,
Episcopal Church, U.S.A.
(adapted)

12   Prayers of the People 3

It is appropriate for a lay person to lead these prayers.

Father, we pray for the holy catholic Church;
that we all may be one.

Grant that every member of the church
may truly and humbly serve you;
that your name may be glorified by all people.

We pray for all ministers of the gospel;
**that they may faithfully proclaim your Word
and administer your holy sacraments.**

We pray for all who govern and hold authority
in the nations of the world;
that there may be justice and peace on the earth.

Give us grace to do your will in all that we undertake;
that our works may find favour in your sight.

Have compassion on those who suffer
from any grief or trouble;
that they may be delivered from their distress.

We praise you for your saints who have entered into joy;
may we also come to share in your heavenly kingdom.

Let us pray for our community,
for the life and worship of this congregation,
and for those whose needs are known to us.

The people offer their own petitions,
either silently or aloud.

Let us pray for ourselves.

After a time of silence,
the leader offers a concluding prayer.

Book of Common Prayer, 1979,
Episcopal Church, U.S.A.
(adapted)

13 A Litany for Advent

In joyful expectation
let us pray to our Saviour and Redeemer,
saying: Lord Jesus, come soon!

O Wisdom, from the mouth of the Most High,
you reign over all things to the ends of the earth,
and dispose them by the power of your love:
come and teach us how to live.
Lord Jesus, come soon!

O Lord, and head of the house of Israel,
you appeared to Moses in the fire of the burning bush,
and you gave the Law on Sinai:
come with outstretched arm and ransom us.
Lord Jesus, come soon!

O Branch of Jesse, standing as a sign among the nations,
all kings will keep silence before you,
and all peoples will summon you to their aid:
come, set us free and delay no more.
Lord Jesus, come soon!

O Key of David and sceptre of the house of Israel,
you open and none can shut;
you shut and none can open:
come and free the captives from prison.
Lord Jesus, come soon!

O Morning Star, splendour of the light eternal
and bright Sun of righteousness:
come and enlighten all who dwell in darkness
and in the shadow of death.
   Lord Jesus, come soon!

O King of the nations, you alone can fulfil their desires:
Cornerstone, you make opposing nations one:
come and save the creature you fashioned from clay.
   Lord Jesus, come soon!

O Emmanuel, hope of the nations and their Saviour:
come and save us, Lord our God.
   Lord Jesus, come soon!

14   A Litany for Christmas

In joy and humility
let us pray to the creator of the universe,
saying: Lord, grant us peace.

By the good news of our salvation
brought to Mary by the angel,
hear us, O Lord.
   Lord, grant us peace.

By the mystery of the Word made flesh,
hear us, O Lord.
   Lord, grant us peace.

By the birth in time
of the timeless Son of God,
hear us, O Lord.
Lord, grant us peace.

By the manifestation of the King of glory
to the shepherds and wise men,
hear us, O Lord.
Lord, grant us peace.

By the submission of the maker of the world
to Mary and Joseph of Nazareth,
hear us, O Lord.
Lord, grant us peace.

By the baptism of the Son of God
in the river Jordan,
hear us, O Lord.
Lord, grant us peace.

Grant that the kingdoms of this world
may become the kingdom of our Lord and Saviour Jesus Christ;
hear us, O Lord.
Lord, grant us peace.

Book of Alternative Services, 1985,
Anglican Church of Canada

15 A Litany for Lent

Let us pray:

**Most holy and merciful God,
we confess to you, and to one another,
that we have sinned by our own fault
in thought, word and deed;
by what we have done,
and by what we have left undone.**

We have not loved you
with our whole heart, and mind, and strength.
We have not loved our neighbours as ourselves.
We have not forgiven others, as we have been forgiven.
Have mercy on us, Lord.

We have been deaf to your call to serve
as Christ served us.
We have not been true to the mind of Christ.
We have grieved the Holy Spirit.
Have mercy on us, Lord.

We confess to you, Lord, all our past unfaithfulness:
our pride, our hypocrisy,
and our failure to be completely honest with ourselves
or with other people;
We confess to you, Lord.

Our preoccupation with our own comforts or possessions,
and our dishonesty in daily life and work;
We confess to you, Lord.

Our exploitation of other people,
and our envy of those with more talents than ourselves;
We confess to you, Lord.

Our negligence in prayer and worship,
and our failure to share the faith we have;
We confess to you, Lord.

Accept our repentance, Lord, for the wrongs we have done:
for our blindness to human need and suffering,
and our indifference to injustice and cruelty;
Accept our repentance, Lord.

For all false judgments,
for uncharitable thoughts toward our neighbours,
and for prejudice and contempt
toward those who differ from us;
Accept our repentance, Lord.

For our waste and pollution of your creation,
and our lack of concern for those who come after us;
Accept our repentance, Lord.

Restore us, good Lord;
Grant us forgiveness and time for amendment of life.

Strengthen us to overcome temptation;
And empower us with the gifts of the Holy Spirit.

By the cross and passion of your Son our Lord,
Bring us with all your saints to the joy of his resurrection.

Book of Common Prayer, 1979,
Episcopal Church, U.S.A.
(adapted)

16   A Litany for Good Friday

Is it nothing to you, all you that pass by?
Look and see if there is any sorrow like my sorrow.

Lamentations 1:12

The Lord says:
My people, what have I done to you?
How have I offended you? Answer me!
I led you from slavery to freedom,
but you led your Saviour to the cross.
I brought you out of Egypt,
but you handed me over to the high priests.
   Holy God,
   holy and mighty, holy and immortal One,
   have mercy on us.

My people, what have I done to you?
How have I offended you? Answer me!
I led you on your way in a pillar of cloud,
but you led me to Pilate's court.
I bore you up with manna in the desert,
but you struck me down and scourged me.
   Holy God,
   holy and mighty, holy and immortal One,
   have mercy on us.

My people, what have I done to you?
How have I offended you? Answer me!
I gave you a royal sceptre,
but you gave me a crown of thorns.
I raised you to the height of majesty,
but you have raised me high on a cross.

**Holy God,
holy and mighty, holy and immortal One,
have mercy on us.**

My people, what have I done to you?
How have I offended you? Answer me!
I gave you saving water from the rock,
but you gave me gall and vinegar to drink.
For you I struck down the kings of Canaan,
but you pierced your Saviour with a lance.
**Holy God,
holy and mighty, holy and immortal One,
have mercy on us.**

We adore you, O Christ, and we bless you.
By your holy cross you have redeemed the world.

If we have died with him, we shall also live with him.
If we endure, we shall also reign with him.

We adore you, O Christ, and we bless you.
By your holy cross you have redeemed the world.

*Adapted from the Reproaches for Good Friday,
Missal of the Roman Catholic Church*

17   A Litany for Easter

In joy and hope
let us pray to the source of all life,
saying: Hear us, Lord of glory!

That our risen Saviour
may fill us with the joy of his holy and life-giving resurrection,
let us pray to the Lord.
Hear us, Lord of glory!

That isolated and persecuted churches
may find fresh strength in the Easter gospel,
let us pray to the Lord.
Hear us, Lord of glory!

That he may grant us humility
to be subject to one another in christian love,
let us pray to the Lord.
Hear us, Lord of glory!

That he may provide
for those who lack food, work, or shelter,
let us pray to the Lord.
Hear us, Lord of glory!

That by his power
wars and famine may cease through all the earth,
let us pray to the Lord.
Hear us, Lord of glory!

That he may reveal the light of his presence
to the sick, the weak, and the dying,
that they may be comforted and strengthened,
let us pray to the Lord.
Hear us, Lord of glory!

That he may send
the fire of the Holy Spirit upon his people,
that we may bear faithful witness to his resurrection,
let us pray to the Lord.
Hear us, Lord of glory!

Book of Alternative Services, 1985,
Anglican Church of Canada

18   A Litany for Pentecost

Let us pray to God the Holy Spirit,
saying: Come, Holy Spirit, come.

Come, Holy Spirit, creator,
and renew the face of the earth.
Come, Holy Spirit, come.

Come, Holy Spirit, counsellor,
and touch our lips that we may proclaim your word.
Come, Holy Spirit, come.

Come, Holy Spirit, power from on high:
make us agents of peace and ministers of wholeness.
Come, Holy Spirit, come.

Come, Holy Spirit, breath of God,
give life to the dry bones of this exiled age,
and make us a living people, holy and free.
Come, Holy Spirit, come.

Come, Holy Spirit, wisdom and truth:
strengthen us in the risk of faith.
Come, Holy Spirit, come.

Book of Alternative Services, 1985,
Anglican Church of Canada

19   A Litany to the Holy Spirit

Holy Spirit,
you are the Lord, the giver of life;
with the Father and the Son we worship and glorify you:
   Come to us now, Spirit of God.

Holy Spirit,
you were there at the creation before time began;
your presence fills the whole universe:
   Come to us now, Spirit of life.

Holy Spirit,
you have spoken through the prophets of old;
by their witness the Word of God has never been silent:
   Come to us now, Spirit of wisdom.

Holy Spirit,
you surrounded the waiting church with the wind of Pentecost;
you gave life and breath to announce Christ's gospel:
   Come to us now, Spirit of power.

Holy Spirit,
you came upon the first christians as a holy fire;
you set their hearts ablaze with devotion to their risen Lord:
   Come to us now, Spirit of love.

Holy Spirit,
you pour out your rich and varied gifts;
you call us to bring forth your fruit in our lives:
   Come to us now, Spirit of grace.

Holy Spirit,
you are the Spirit of truth, the Counsellor;
you lead us to the truth that sets us free:
   Come to us now, Spirit of God,
   and renew Christ's holy church.

20   A Litany of the Evening

In peace let us pray to the Lord,
saying: We pray to you, Lord.

That this evening may be holy, good, and peaceful:
We pray to you, Lord.

That the work we have done this day
and the people we have met
may bring us closer to you:
We pray to you, Lord.

That we may be forgiven our sins and offences:
We pray to you, Lord.

That we may hear and respond
to your call to peace and justice:
We pray to you, Lord.

That you will sustain the faith and hope
of the weary, the lonely, and the oppressed:
We pray to you, Lord.

That you will strengthen us in your service,
and fill our hearts with longing for your kingdom:
We pray to you, Lord.

21 A Litany of the Late Evening

Keep us, O Lord, as the apple of your eye.
Hide us under the shadow of your wings.

For the peace of the whole world,
we pray to you, Lord.
Lord, have mercy.

For those who are weary, sleepless, and depressed,
we pray to you, Lord.
Lord, have mercy.

For those who are hungry, sick, and frightened,
we pray to you, Lord.
Lord, have mercy.

For rest and refreshment,
we pray to you, Lord.
Lord, have mercy.

Guide us waking, O Lord,
and guard us sleeping;

that awake we may watch with Christ,
and asleep we may rest in peace. Amen.

Book of Alternative Services, 1985,
Anglican Church of Canada

22 The Great Cloud of Witnesses

We give thanks to you, O Lord our God,
for all your servants and witnesses of time past:

For Abraham, the father of believers, and Sarah his wife,
for Moses, the lawgiver, and Aaron, the priest;
We give you thanks, O Lord.

For Miriam and Joshua, Deborah and Gideon,
for Samuel, with Hannah his mother;
We give you thanks, O Lord.

For David, king and psalmist of Israel,
for Isaiah and all the prophets;
We give you thanks, O Lord.

For Mary, the mother of our Lord,
for Joseph, Elizabeth and John the Baptist;
We give you thanks, O Lord.

For Peter and Paul and all the apostles,
for Mary and Martha, and Mary Magdalene;
We give you thanks, O Lord.

For Stephen, the first martyr,
for all the martyrs and saints and faithful witnesses
in every age and in every land;
We give you thanks, O Lord.

That you have called us all to be your saints
and have numbered us among your chosen people:
We give you thanks, O Lord.

In your mercy, O Lord our God,
give us, as you give to all the faithful,
the hope of salvation and the promise of eternal life;
through Jesus Christ our Lord,
the first-born of many from the dead.
Amen.

Book of Common Prayer, 1979,
Episcopal Church, U.S.A.
(adapted)

23   A Litany for a Church Anniversary

Brothers and sisters,
we rejoice that the Holy Spirit inspired our forebears
to form this congregation for God's praise
and to build this sanctuary to God's glory.
On this joyful occasion of our . . . church anniversary,
let us pray to the Lord:

I   Prayer of Thanksgiving

Eternal and loving God,
today we give thanks to you for your goodness
through all the years of worship and witness in this place.

For your grace in calling us to be your people;
for your love revealed to us in Christ your Son;
for your gift of the Spirit and the joy of salvation:
   We give you our thanks, O God.

For those who established the church here:
for their faith and vision,
for their gifts and abilities:
   We give you our thanks, O God.

For all who have been members of this church;
for those who have given freely of their time and money;
for those whose wisdom guided our congregation:
   We give you our thanks, O God.

For all who have preached and taught here;
for all who have confessed here that Jesus is Lord;
for all who today lead in worship, witness, and service:
   We give you our thanks, O God. Amen.

II

The people stand

And now let us reaffirm our loyalty to Christ
and pledge our faithfulness to the church:

That God may be reverently worshipped;
that the gospel may be faithfully proclaimed;
that the sacraments may be joyfully celebrated:
   We pledge our allegiance to Christ and the church.

That our families and friendships may be enriched;
that our daily lives and work may be consecrated;
that our faith and love may be nurtured:
   We pledge our allegiance to Christ and the church.

For the teaching and guiding of those who are young;
for the encouraging and equipping of those who serve;
for the strengthening of those who seek God's way;
and for the comforting of those who mourn:
   We pledge our allegiance to Christ and the church.

For the conversion of the world to our Saviour;
for the reconciliation of people and nations;
for the promotion of righteousness and peace;
and for the extension of the reign of God:
   We pledge our allegiance to Christ and the church.

In loving remembrance of all who have run the race
and finished their course;
in gratitude for one another here today
who make up the body of Christ in this place;
in thanksgiving for all who keep the faith
and in communion with all God's people on earth:
   We pledge our allegiance to Christ and the church. Amen.

Vestry Prayers

With the Minister or Leader of Worship

1   Eternal God,
     help us to remember your presence with us now
     as we lead the worship of your people;
     and may their hearts and ours be lifted up
     in humble prayer and joyful praise,
     to the glory of our Lord Jesus Christ.

2   Almighty God,
     through the ages you have given ministers to your church
     that your people may be nourished in faith
     and equipped for service.
     Now bless your servant N
     as he/she leads the worship of your people here
     and proclaims your gospel today;
     through Jesus Christ our Lord.

3   Grant, O God,
     that as we lead the praise of others
     we may ourselves gladly and thankfully worship you;
     and help us, as we lead the prayers of others,
     to come before you with reverent and prayerful spirit;
     so that the words of our mouth
     and the meditation of our hearts
     may be acceptable in your sight;
     through Jesus Christ our Lord.

4   Prepare us, O God, for the worship of your house,
    and give us grace to serve you with reverence,
    joy and thanksgiving;
    through Jesus Christ our Lord.

5   We thank you, O God, for the privilege of worship
    and pray your blessing on all who gather here today.
    May your servant N know the guidance
    and strengthening power of the Holy Spirit
    as he/she leads us now.
    May we all be very conscious of your presence with us
    and of our unity with all who worship you this day;
    through Jesus Christ our Lord.

6   O God,
    grant that I/we may help the worship of your people
    by my/our sincerity;
    for the sake of Jesus Christ my/our Lord.

7   Eternal God,
    for ever worshipped in heaven and on earth,
    may our worship today be a joyful offering to you.
    As we draw near to you in praise and prayer
    and as your gospel is proclaimed,
    may the sad or weary find comfort,
    the weak find strength,
    and the strong find confirmation and challenge.
    May all be for your glory, O God,
    through Jesus Christ our Lord.

With the Choir

8   Open our lips, O Lord;
    and our mouth shall proclaim your praise.

9   O God,
    you have given us minds to know you,
    hearts to love you,
    and voices to show forth your praise.
    Help us to worship you with understanding,
    reverence and joy;
    and grant that, in this service,
    we may both receive your blessing
    and be made a blessing to others;
    for the sake of Jesus Christ our Lord.

10   Serve the Lord with gladness;
    come before his presence with a song.
    Proclaim with me the greatness of the Lord;
    let us exalt his name together.

11   O God,
    you alone are worthy of all praise.
    Inspire and help us by the Holy Spirit
    that, as we join in worship now,
    the words on our lips, the thoughts in our minds,
    and the prayers in our hearts
    may be a worthy offering to you, our God.
    May all be done for the glory of your name;
    through Jesus Christ our Lord.

12 Enable us, O God,
    to lift our hearts with our voices
    as we sing your praise,
    that in all things we may glorify your name;
    through Jesus Christ our Lord.

13 O Lord,
    open our lips and tune our hearts to sing your praise;
    and make us now and always worthy of your service;
    for Jesus Christ's sake.

14 Praise the Lord,
    sing his praise in the congregation of the faithful.
      We will be glad and rejoice in God;
      we will sing praises to his name.

15 Holy God,
    you have called us to serve you
    in the worship of your house.
    Grant us so to praise you
    with our hearts as with our voices,
    that the souls of all assembled with us
    may be uplifted, purified and strengthened;
    and that they and we together
    may be confirmed in faith and love to you;
    through Jesus Christ our Lord.

16 Sing to the Lord;
    lift up your voice, rejoice and sing.
      How good it is to sing praises to our God.
      Praise the Lord!

17 Almighty God,
    you have given us the gift of music
    to enrich our human lives
    and to be used for your praise.
    May the music we offer here today
    be true and acceptable worship;
    through Jesus Christ our Lord.

18 Let my cry come before you, O Lord;
    give me understanding, according to your word.
    My tongue shall sing of your promise;
    my lips shall pour forth your praise.
    I will be glad and rejoice in you;
    I will sing to your name, O Most High.

19 Grant us your blessing, O God,
    as we lead your people in this service today.
    We offer this time of worship to you,
    in the name of Jesus.

20 O Lord our God,
    worshipped in heaven and on earth,
    bless those who sing in this choir today.
    Give them sincerity and reverence,
    that what they sing with their voices
    may be the offering of their hearts;
    to the honour and glory of your name.

A Treasury of Prayers

1   The Lord's Prayer

Our Father in heaven,
  hallowed be your name,
  your kingdom come,
  your will be done,
    on earth as in heaven.
Give us today our daily bread.
Forgive us our sins
  as we forgive those who sin against us.
Save us from the time of trial
  and deliver us from evil.

For the kingdom, the power, and the glory are yours
  now and for ever. Amen.

Matthew 6:9-13

Alternative Version

Our Father, who art in heaven,
  hallowed be thy name,
  thy kingdom come,
  thy will be done,
    on earth as it is in heaven.
Give us this day our daily bread.
And forgive us our trespasses,
  as we forgive those who trespass against us.
And lead us not into temptation,
  but deliver us from evil.

For thine is the kingdom, the power and the glory,
  for ever and ever. Amen.

Matthew 6:9-13

2   Prayer over the Bread and Wine

We give you thanks, O Father,
for the life and knowledge
which you have made known to us
through your Son Jesus;
yours is the glory for ever and ever.
As the grain once scattered in the fields
and the grapes once dispersed on the hillside
are now united on this table in bread and wine,
so, Lord, may your whole church soon be gathered together
from the ends of the earth into your kingdom;
for yours is the glory and power,
through Jesus Christ, for ever and ever. Amen.

From the Didache, 2nd century

3   For the Answering of our Prayers

Almighty God,
you have given us grace at this time with one accord
to make our common supplications to you;
and you have promised, through your well-beloved Son,
that when two or three are gathered together in his name
you will be in the midst of them:
Fulfil now, O Lord, our desires and petitions
as may be best for us;
granting us in this world knowledge of your truth,
and in the age to come life everlasting. Amen.

St John Chrysostom, 347-407

4 Abiding in God

O loving God,
to turn away from you is to fall,
to turn towards you is to rise,
and to stand before you is to abide for ever.
Grant us, dear God,
in all our duties your help;
in all our uncertainties your guidance;
in all our dangers your protection;
and in all our sorrows your peace;
through Jesus Christ our Lord. Amen.

St Augustine, 354-430

5 The Shield of God

May the strength of God pilot us.
May the power of God preserve us.
May the wisdom of God instruct us.
May the hand of God protect us.
May the way of God direct us.
May the shield of God defend us.
May the host of God
  guard us against the snares of evil
  and the temptations of the world.

May Christ be with us,
Christ before us,
Christ in us,
Christ over us.
May your salvation, O Lord, be always ours,
this day and for evermore. Amen.

Part of the 'Breastplate' of St Patrick, 389-461

6   Prayer After Receiving Holy Communion

Grant, O Lord Jesus,
that the ears which have heard the voice of your songs
may be closed to the voice of dispute;
that the eyes which have seen your great love
may also behold your blessed hope;
that the tongues which have sung your praise
may speak the truth in love;
that the feet which have walked in your courts
may walk in the region of light;
and that the bodies which have received your living body
may be restored in newness of life.
Glory to you for your inexpressible gift. Amen.

Liturgy of Malabar, 5th century

7   For the Ministry of Healing

O Lord and Master Jesus Christ,
Word of the everlasting Father,
you have borne our griefs
and carried the burdens of our human frailty;
by the power of the Holy Spirit,
renew in your church the gifts of healing,
and send out your disciples again
to preach the gospel of your kingdom,
to heal the sick,
and to relieve the sufferings of your children;
to the praise and glory of your holy name. Amen.

Liturgy of St Mark, 5th century

8   Seeking the Lord

O gracious and holy God,
give us diligence to seek you,
wisdom to perceive you,
and patience to wait for you.

Grant us, O God,
a mind to meditate on you;
eyes to behold you;
ears to listen for your word;
a heart to love you;
and a life to proclaim you;
through the power of the Spirit
of Jesus Christ our Lord. Amen.

St Benedict, 480-543

9   For Protection Through the Night

Be present, O merciful God,
and protect us through the silent hours of this night;
so that we, who are wearied by the changes and chances
of this fleeting world,
may repose upon thy eternal changelessness;
through Jesus Christ our Lord. Amen.

Leonine Sacramentary, 6th century

10   The Freedom of Serving God

O loving God,
you are the light of the minds that know you,
the life of the souls that love you,
and the strength of the hearts that serve you.

Help us so to know you
that we may truly love you;
and so to love you
that we may faithfully serve you,
whom to serve is perfect freedom;
through Jesus Christ our Lord. Amen.

Gelasian Sacramentary, 7th century

11   The Salvation of the Whole World

O God of unchangeable power and eternal light,
look favourably on your whole church,
that wonderful and sacred mystery;
and by the peaceful operation of your providence,
carry out the work of our salvation.
And let the whole world feel and see
that things which were cast down are being raised up,
and things which had grown old are being made new,
and all things are returning to perfection
through him from whom they took their origin;
even through our Lord Jesus Christ. Amen.

Gelasian Sacramentary, 7th century

12   For Forgiveness and Strength

Almighty and merciful God,
the fountain of all goodness,
you know the thoughts of our hearts:
we confess that we have sinned against you
and done what is evil in your sight.
Wash us from the stains of our past sins,
and give us grace and power to put away all hurtful things,
so that, being delivered from the bondage of sin,
we may bring forth fruits worthy of repentance.

O eternal Light, shine into our hearts;
eternal Goodness, deliver us from evil;
O eternal Power, give us your strength;
eternal Wisdom, scatter the darkness of our ignorance;
O eternal Pity, have mercy on us.

Grant that with all our hearts, and minds, and strength
we may always seek your face;
and finally, in your infinite mercy,
bring us to your holy presence.
So strengthen our weakness
that, following in the footsteps of your blessed Son,
we may obtain your mercy,
and enter into your promised joy. Amen.

Alcuin, 735-804

13   For the Graces of the Holy Spirit

O merciful God,
fill our hearts with the graces of the Holy Spirit,
with love, joy, peace,
patience, kindness, goodness,
faithfulness, gentleness and self-control.
Teach us to love those who hate us,
to bless those who curse us,
and to pray for those who abuse us,
that we may be the children of our Father:
who makes the sun shine on the evil and the good,
and sends rain on the just and unjust.
In adversity grant us grace to be patient;
in prosperity keep us humble;
may we guard the door of our lips;

may we lightly regard the pleasures of this world,
and thirst only after heavenly things;
through Jesus Christ our Lord. Amen.

St Anselm, 1033-1109

14 Jesus, Redeemer and Brother

Praise be to you, my Lord Jesus Christ,
for all the benefits
you have won for me,
for all the pains and insults
you have borne for me.

O most merciful Redeemer,
friend and brother,
may I know you more clearly,
love you more dearly,
and follow you more nearly,
day by day. Amen.

St Richard of Chichester, 1197-1253

15 For Enlightenment of the Mind

Enlighten us, O good Jesus,
with the brightness of internal light,
and cast out all darkness
from the dwelling of our hearts.
Grant us, O Lord,
to know that which is worth knowing,
to love what is worth loving,

to praise that which can bear with praise,
to hate what in your sight is unworthy,
to prize what to you is precious,
and above all,
to search out and do your holy will. Amen.

Thomas a Kempis, 1380-1471

16   The Way, the Truth, and the Life

Lord Jesus Christ,
you have said that you are the Way,
the Truth and the Life:
do not let us at any time stray from you,
for you are our Way;
or ever distrust your promises,
for you are our Truth;
or ever rest in anything other than you,
for you are our Life.

Lord Jesus,
you have taught us
what to believe,
what to do,
what to hope for,
and in whom to take our rest. Amen.

Erasmus, 1466-1536

17   A Prayer of Commitment

Teach us, good Lord,
to serve you as you deserve:
to give, and not to count the cost;

to fight, and not to heed the wounds;
to toil, and not to seek for rest;
to labour, and not to ask for any reward,
except that of knowing that we do your holy will;
through Jesus Christ our Lord. Amen.

Ignatius Loyola, 1491-1556

18 A Prayer For Illumination

Most gracious God, our heavenly Father,
in you alone dwells all fullness of light and wisdom:
illuminate our minds by the Holy Spirit
in the true understanding of your Word.
Give us grace that we may receive it
with sincere reverence and humility.
May it lead us to put our whole trust in you alone;
and so to serve and honour you
that we may glorify your name,
and encourage others by the good example
of a holy life.
And because it has pleased you to number us
among your people,
help us to give you the love and homage that we owe,
as children of the light and as servants to our Lord.
We ask this for the sake of our Master and Saviour. Amen.

John Calvin, 1509-1564

19 To Walk with a Perfect Heart

Lord,
for thy tender mercies' sake,
lay not our sins to our charge,

but forgive that which is past
and give us grace to amend our lives;
to decline from sin and incline to virtue,
that we may walk with a perfect heart before thee,
now and evermore. Amen.

Ridley's Prayers, 1566

20   For the Holy Catholic Church

Gracious Father,
we humbly beseech thee for thy holy catholic Church.
Fill it with all truth;
and in all truth with all peace.
Where it is corrupt, purge it;
where it is in error, direct it;
where it is superstitious, rectify it;
where anything is amiss, reform it;
where it is right, strengthen and confirm it;
where it is in want, furnish it;
where it is divided and rent assunder,
make up the breaches of it, O thou Holy One of Israel;
for the sake of Jesus Christ our Lord and Saviour. Amen.

Archbishop William Laud, 1573-1645

21   For the Renewal of our Hearts

Instruct our mouths, O Lord, with a new song;
that, our hearts being renewed,
we may always rejoice in thy praise
and in the company of thy saints,
O God, our Strength and our Redeemer. Amen.

Ancient Scottish Prayers, 1595

22 Offering Ourselves to God

O God,
who hast so greatly loved us,
long sought us,
and mercifully redeemed us;
give us grace that in everything
we may yield ourselves,
our wills and our works,
a continual thankoffering unto thee;
through Jesus Christ our Lord. Amen.

Westminster Divines, 1647

23 For the Right Use of Scripture

Blessed Lord,
who hast caused all holy Scriptures
to be written for our learning:
grant that we may in such wise hear them,
read, mark, learn and inwardly digest them,
that by patience, and comfort of thy holy Word,
we may embrace, and ever hold fast
the blessed hope of everlasting life,
which thou hast given us in our Saviour Jesus Christ. Amen.

Book of Common Prayer, 1662,
Church of England

24 Preparing God's Way

O Lord Jesu Christ,
who at thy first coming didst send thy messenger
to prepare thy way before thee:

grant that the ministers and stewards of thy mysteries
may likewise so prepare and make ready thy way,
by turning the hearts of the disobedient
to the wisdom of the just,
that at thy second coming to judge the world
we may be found an acceptable people in thy sight,
who livest and reignest with the Father and the Holy Spirit,
ever one God, world without end. Amen.

Book of Common Prayer, 1662

25 God's Strength and Protection

O God,
who knowest us to be set in the midst
of so many and great dangers,
that by reason of the frailty of our nature
we cannot always stand upright:
grant to us such strength and protection,
as may support us in all dangers,
and carry us through all temptations;
through Jesus Christ our Lord. Amen.

Book of Common Prayer, 1662

26 For Steadfast Hearts

Almighty God,
who alone canst order the unruly wills and affections
of sinful men:
grant unto thy people,
that they may love the things which thou commandest,
and desire that which thou dost promise;

that so, among the sundry and manifold changes
of the world,
our hearts may surely there be fixed
where true joys are to be found;
through Jesus Christ our Lord. Amen.

Book of Common Prayer, 1662

27   For the Help of God's Grace

O God,
the strength of all them that put their trust in thee,
mercifully accept our prayers;
and because through the weakness of our mortal nature
we can do no good thing without thee,
grant us the help of thy grace,
that in keeping of thy commandments we may please thee,
both in will and deed;
through Jesus Christ our Lord. Amen.

Book of Common Prayer, 1662

28   Loving God Above All Things

O God,
who hast prepared for them that love thee
such good things as pass man's understanding:
pour into our hearts such love toward thee,
that we, loving thee above all things,
may obtain thy promises,
which exceed all that we can desire;
through Jesus Christ our Lord. Amen.

Book of Common Prayer, 1662

29   The Love of God's Name

Lord of all power and might,
who art the author and giver of all good things:
graft in our hearts the love of thy name,
increase in us true religion,
nourish us with all goodness,
and of thy great mercy keep us in the same;
through Jesus Christ our Lord. Amen.

Book of Common Prayer, 1662

30   The Abundance of God's Mercy

Almighty and everlasting God,
who art always more ready to hear than we to pray,
and art wont to give
more than either we desire, or deserve:
pour down upon us the abundance of thy mercy;
forgiving us those things
whereof our conscience is afraid,
and giving us those good things
which we are not worthy to ask,
but through the merits and mediation of Jesus Christ,
thy Son, our Lord. Amen.

Book of Common Prayer, 1662

31   The Holy Spirit's Guidance

O God,
forasmuch as without thee
we are not able to please thee:

mercifully grant that thy Holy Spirit
may in all things direct and rule our hearts;
through Jesus Christ our Lord. Amen.

Book of Common Prayer, 1662

32 For Freedom from Fear

O God,
who art the author of peace and lover of concord,
in knowledge of whom standeth our eternal life,
whose service is perfect freedom:
defend us thy humble servants
in all assaults of our enemies;
that we, surely trusting in thy defence,
may not fear the power of any adversaries,
through the might of Jesus Christ our Lord. Amen.

Book of Common Prayer, 1662

33 A Prayer for the Lord's Day

Eternal and most glorious God,
you dwell in light which no one can approach,
and live and reign for ever and ever:
we bless you that you have brought us by your grace
to see the light of another day.
Help us, O Lord, this day
to commemorate the rising of our blessed Redeemer;
and let our hearts be raised to the heavenly world,
and to Jesus, who sits at your right hand in glory.

May the blessed Holy Spirit visit us with divine influence,
and remain with us in both public and private worship,
for without the blessed Spirit's gracious assistance,
we can do nothing that is acceptable to you.

May we attend with cheerfulness and holy desire
on the ordinances of your house this day,
and may we find your presence in the assembly of your people.
May our souls be lifted up to you
in the prayers that will be offered,
and may our lips sing your praises with holy joy.
Let us come away from your house
under the light of your countenance,
satisfied with your love
declared to the world in Christ Jesus our Lord. Amen.

Isaac Watts, 1674-1748 (abridged)

34   The Holy Love of God

Deliver us, O God,
from a lazy mind,
all lukewarmness of heart,
and all depression of spirit.
We know that these must deaden our love for you;
mercifully free our hearts from them all.
And give us such a lively, fervent and cheerful spirit
that we may vigorously perform whatever you command,
thankfully suffer whatever you choose for us,
and always be eager to obey your holy love
in all things;
through Jesus Christ our Lord. Amen.

John Wesley, 1703-1791

35 An Instrument of God's Peace

Lord, make me an instrument of your peace;
where there is hatred, let me sow love;
where there is injury, pardon;
where there is discord, union;
where there is doubt, faith;
where there is despair, hope;
where there is darkness, light;
where there is sadness, joy;
for your mercy and truth's sake.

O divine Master,
grant that I may not so much seek
to be consoled as to console,
to be understood as to understand,
to be loved as to love.
For it is in giving that we receive;
it is in pardoning that we are pardoned;
it is in dying that we are born to eternal life. Amen.

A 19th century prayer in the spirit
of St Francis of Assisi

36 The Flame of Faith

Almighty God,
let not the flame of faith,
once kindled in our hearts,
be quenched for ever;
but do thou continually feed and renew it,
that it may ever shine amid our darkness and groping,
until thou dost bring us to eternal light;
through Jesus Christ our Lord. Amen.

Presbyterian Forms of Service, 1899

37   For Guidance by God's Word and Spirit

Eternal and ever-blessed God,
who art the Author of our life
and the End of our pilgrimage;
we beseech thee so to guide us by thy Word and Spirit
amid all perils and temptations,
that we may not wander from thy way,
nor stumble upon dark mountains;
but may finish our course in safety,
and come to our eternal rest in thee;
through the grace and merit
of Jesus Christ our Lord. Amen.

Book of Common Worship, 1908

38   A Prayer for the Inland

Lift our eyes, O Father,
that we may see our fellow citizens
even to the furthermost shores of our continent.
Quicken our imagination
until their lives become clear to us.
Call to our remembrance
our own struggles and difficulties when isolated,
our own sighings when in loneliness.
Open our hearts,
that our love may flow out in warm streams of blessing,
expressed in things both seen and unseen.

Keep and enable all whom we have sent forth in thy name.
Follow our pioneers through all their days:
in the midst of drought or flood, keep them from harm;
in the days of loss, give them patience;
in time of temptation, strength;
in the season of pain, joy.

Especially we ask thee to bless the children
in isolated homes:
enrich their lives, and make them great;
let thy protecting wings cover them;
may the Holy Spirit –
who knows no distance, no time, no barrier –
comfort, inspire and perfect them.

Let the love of thy Son flow about us all
and bring us to the rest of thy eternal kingdom;
through Jesus Christ our Lord. Amen.

A prayer written in 1915 by the Revd John
Flynn, 1880-1951, the founder of the
Australian Inland Mission and the
Royal Flying Doctor Service.

39   The Heavenly Food of God's Word

O God,
who hast so made us that we live not by bread alone,
but by every word of God;
and who hast taught us not to spend our labour
on that which cannot satisfy;
cause us to hunger after the heavenly food of thy Word,
and to find in it our daily provision
on the way to eternal life;
through Jesus Christ our Lord. Amen.

Prayers for Divine Service, 1923, Church of Scotland

40   For Those from Whom We are Separated

O Lord our God,
who art in every place,
and from whom no space or distance can ever part us;
take into thy holy keeping
those from whom we are now separated;
and grant that both they and we,
by drawing nearer to thee,
may be drawn nearer to one another,
in Jesus Christ our Lord. Amen.

Book of Common Order, 1940, Church of Scotland

41   In Praise of the Trinity

Glory be to thee, O Father everlasting,
who didst send thine only begotten Son into the world
that we might live through him.
Glory be to thee, O Lord Jesus Christ,
who hast brought life and immortality to light
through the gospel.
Glory be to thee, O Holy Spirit of God,
who dost quicken us together with Christ,
and dost shed abroad his love in our hearts.
Blessed be thou,
Father, Son, and Holy Spirit, one God;
and blessed be thy glorious name for ever. Amen.

Book of Common Order, 1940, Church of Scotland

42 For the Knowledge of God's Will

Almighty and everlasting God,
in whom we live and move and have our being,
who hast created us for thyself,
so that we can find rest only in thee;
grant unto us such purity of heart
and strength of purpose,
that no selfish passion may hinder us
from knowing thy will,
no weakness from doing it;
but in thy light we may see light clearly,
and in thy service find perfect freedom;
for Jesus Christ's sake. Amen.

Book of Common Order, 1940, Church of Scotland

43 This Bundle of Life

O God,
who hast bound us together in this bundle of life,
give us grace to understand
how our lives depend upon the courage, the industry,
the honesty and the integrity of our fellow-men;
that we may be mindful of their needs,
grateful for their faithfulness,
and faithful to our responsibilities to them;
through Jesus Christ our Lord. Amen.

Reinhold Niebuhr, 1892-1971

44 The Workshop of the Carpenter

O Christ, the Master Carpenter,
who at the last through wood and nails
purchased our whole salvation;
wield well your tools in the workshop of your world,
so that we, who come rough-hewn to your bench,
may here be fashioned to a truer beauty by your hand.
We ask this in your name and for your sake. Amen.

A prayer of the Iona Community, Scotland

45 For Strength Through the Day

Great Bunji God,
you sent your Son Jesus
to be our Saviour, our Guide and our Friend.
At the dawn of this new day
we pray for strength to follow in his steps,
and to be true witnesses for him
among our people who love the great earth mother,
your gift to them from the dreamtime.
We pray for all people of all countries,
that they may become one great family
with Jesus as Saviour.
As we come to the evening of this day,
may we go to our rest in the quiet hours of the night
knowing that, in spite of our human weaknesses,
we have truly walked with Jesus.
This prayer we offer in the name of Jesus,
our Good Friend. Aralba.

Revd Lazarus Lamilami, 1910-1977,
the first ordained Aboriginal minister
of the Uniting Church

Bunji is an Aboriginal word for Father.
Aralba means: I have spoken from my heart.

46 Bearers of Reconciliation

Lord Christ,
at times we are like strangers on this earth,
disconcerted by all the violence and harsh oppositions.
Like a gentle breeze,
you breathe upon us the Spirit of peace.
Transfigure the deserts of our doubts
and so prepare us to be bearers of reconciliation
wherever you place us,
that the hope of peace may arise in our world. Amen.

Brother Roger of Taize, 1915-

47 For Prisoners of Conscience

Lord Jesus,
you experienced the sufferings and the death
of a prisoner of conscience.
You yourself were plotted against,
betrayed by a friend,
and arrested under cover of darkness.
You were tortured, beaten and humiliated,
and sentenced to an agonising death,
although you had done no wrong.
Be now with prisoners of conscience throughout the world.
Be with them in the darkness of the dungeon,
in the loneliness of separation from those they love;
be with them in their fear of what may happen to them,
in the agony of their torture,
and in the face of execution and death.

Stretch out your hands in power
to break their chains and to open the gates of freedom,
that your kingdom of justice
may be established now among them. Amen.

Commission for Mission
Prayer Fellowship Handbook

48   The Collect for Purity

Modern Version

Almighty God,
to whom all hearts are open,
all desires known,
and from whom no secrets are hidden:
cleanse the thoughts of our hearts
by the inspiration of your Holy Spirit,
that we may perfectly love you,
and worthily magnify your holy name;
through Christ our Lord. Amen.

Alternative Service Book, 1980,
Church of England

Traditional Version

Almighty God,
unto whom all hearts be open,
all desires known,
and from whom no secrets are hid:
cleanse the thoughts of our hearts
by the inspiration of thy Holy Spirit,
that we may perfectly love thee,
and worthily magnify thy holy name;
through Christ our Lord. Amen.

Gregorian Sacramentary, 590

49 A General Confession

Almighty and most merciful Father,
we have strayed from your ways like lost sheep.
We have left undone what we ought to have done,
and we have done what we ought not to have done.
We have followed our own ways
and the desires of our own hearts.
We have broken your holy laws.
Yet, good Lord, have mercy on us;
restore those who are penitent,
according to your promises declared to all people
in Jesus Christ our Lord.
And grant, merciful Father, for his sake,
that we may live a godly and obedient life,
to the glory of your holy name. Amen.

An Australian Prayer Book, 1978,
Anglican Church of Australia

50 A General Thanksgiving

Almighty God, Father of all mercies,
we your unworthy servants give you humble thanks
for all your goodness and loving-kindness
to us and all whom you have made.
We bless you for our creation, preservation,
and all the blessings of this life;
but above all for your immeasurable love
in the redemption of the world by our Lord Jesus Christ;
for the means of grace, and for the hope of glory.
And, we pray, give us such an awareness of your mercies,
that with truly thankful hearts

we may show forth your praise,
not only with our lips, but in our lives,
by giving up ourselves to your service,
and by walking before you
in holiness and righteousness all our days;
through Jesus Christ our Lord,
to whom with you and the Holy Spirit
be honour and glory throughout all ages. Amen.

Book of Common Prayer, 1979,
Episcopal Church, U.S.A.

51   The Prayer of Humble Access

Modern Version

We do not presume
to come to your table, merciful Lord,
trusting in our own righteousness,
but in your manifold and great mercies.
We are not worthy
so much as to gather up the crumbs under your table.
But you are the same Lord
whose nature is always to have mercy.
Grant us, therefore, gracious Lord,
so to eat the flesh of your dear Son Jesus Christ,
and to drink his blood,
that we may evermore dwell in him,
and he in us. Amen.

An Australian Prayer Book, 1978,
Anglican Church of Australia

We do not presume
to come to this thy table, O merciful Lord,
trusting in our own righteousness,
but in thy manifold and great mercies.
We are not worthy
so much as to gather up the crumbs under thy table.
But thou art the same Lord
whose property is always to have mercy.
Grant us, therefore, gracious Lord,
so to eat the flesh of thy dear Son Jesus Christ,
and to drink his blood,
that our sinful bodies may be made clean by his body,
and our souls washed through his most precious blood,
and that we may evermore dwell in him,
and he in us. Amen.

Book of Common Prayer, 1662,
Church of England

52 For the Peace which the World Cannot Give

Eternal God,
from whom all holy desires,
all good purposes, and all just works proceed:
give to your servants that peace
which the world cannot give,
that our hearts may be set to obey your commandments,
and that free from the fear of our enemies
we may pass our time in trust and quietness;
through the merits of Jesus Christ our Saviour. Amen.

An Australian Prayer Book, 1978

53   A Collect of the Morning

Lord our heavenly Father,
almighty and everlasting God,
we thank you for bringing us safely to this day.
Keep us by your mighty power,
and grant that today we fall into no sin,
neither run into any kind of danger,
but lead and govern us in all things,
that we may always do what is righteous in your sight;
through Jesus Christ our Lord. Amen.

An Australian Prayer Book, 1978

54   A Collect of the Evening

Lighten our darkness,
Lord, we pray;
and in your great mercy defend us
from all perils and dangers of this night;
for the love of your only Son,
our Saviour Jesus Christ. Amen.

An Australian Prayer Book, 1978

55   For Unity with all God's Children

Confront us, O Christ,
with the hidden prejudices and fears
which deny and betray our prayers.
Enable us to see the causes of strife;
remove from us all false sense of superiority.
Teach us to grow in unity with all God's children.
Into your hands, O Lord,
we commend all for whom we pray,
trusting in your mercy now and for ever. Amen.

World Council of Churches 6th Assembly, 1983,
Vancouver

56   A Rolling Brown Land

Lord God,
your Spirit has moved over the face of Australia
and formed from its dust a rolling brown land.
Your Spirit has moved over its warm tropical waters
and created a rich variety of life.
Your Spirit has moved in the lives
of men, women, and children
and given them, from the dreamtime,
an affinity with their lands and waters.
Your Spirit has moved in pilgrim people
and brought them to a place of freedom and plenty.
Your Spirit moves still today
in sprawling, high-rise cities,
in the vast distances of the outback,
and in the ethnic diversity of the Australian people.

Lord God,
in the midst of this varied huddle of humanity
you have set your church.
Give us, the people you have so richly blessed,
a commitment to justice and peace for all nations;
and a vision of righteousness
and equality for all people in our own country.
Help us look beyond our far horizons
to see our neighbours in their many guises,
so that we may be mutually enriched by our differences.
And may our love and compassion for all people on earth
be as wide and varied as our land
and as constant as the grace of our Lord, Jesus Christ. Amen.

The Revd Douglas McKenzie

Sentence Prayers

Eternal God,
you are our dwelling place,
and underneath are your everlasting arms.

Deuteronomy 33:27

Bless the Lord, O my soul,
and all that is within me, bless his holy name.

Psalm 103:1

Lord, I believe: help my unbelief.

The father of the epileptic boy,
Mark 9:24

Behold, I am the servant of the Lord;
let it be to me according to your word.

Mary of Nazareth, Luke 1:38

Lord, teach us to pray.

The disciples of Jesus, Luke 11:1

Father,
I haved sinned against heaven and before you;
I am no longer worthy to be called your son.

The Prodigal Son, Luke 15:21

God, be merciful to me, a sinner.

The tax collector, Luke 18:13

Jesus, remember me
when you come in your kingly power.

One of the criminals on Good Friday,
Luke 23:42

Stay with us, Lord,
for it is toward evening
and the day is now far spent.

The two at the home at Emmaus,
Luke 24:29

Lord, give us this bread always.

The people at Capernaum, John 6:34

Lord, to whom shall we go?
You have the words of eternal life.

The disciple Simon Peter, John 6:68

Lord, show us the Father,
and we shall be satisfied.

The disciple Philip, John 14:18

My Lord and my God.

The disciple Thomas, John 20:28

Lord, you know everything;
you know that I love you.

The disciple Simon Peter, John 21:17

O Lord,
direct our hearts to the love of God
and the endurance of Christ.

The apostle Paul, 2 Thessalonians 3:5

Amen. Come, Lord Jesus.

God's servant John, Revelation 22:20

In the name of the Father,
and of the Son,
and of the Holy Spirit. Amen.

The early church

Lord Jesus Christ, Son of God,
have mercy on me, a sinner.

The 'Jesus Prayer' of the Orthodox Church

O God,
make us children of quietness,
and heirs of Christ's peace.

St Clement, died A.D. 95

My past life hide; my future guide.
(Quod vixi tege; quod vivam rege.)

Author unknown

Guide us waking, O Lord,
and guard us sleeping;
that awake we may watch with Christ,
and asleep we may rest in peace.

The office of Compline

O Lord who lends us life,
lend us a heart replete with thankfulness.

William Shakespeare, 1564-1616

Lord,
let your glory be my end,
your word my rule,
and then your will be done.

King Charles 1, 1600-1649

Lord,
you know how busy I must be today;
if I should forget you,
please do not forget me.

*Sir Jacob Astley, before the battle
of Edgehill, 1642*

O God,
help me not to despise or oppose
what I do not understand.

William Penn, 1644-1718

O Lord,
let me not live to be useless,
for Christ's sake.

John Wesley, 1703-1791

I know you,
I love you,
I will work for you, Lord Jesus.

Author unknown

Lord,
give us faith that right makes might.

Abraham Lincoln, 1809-1865

O Saviour of the world,
who by thy cross and precious blood
hast redeemed us;
save us and help us,
we humbly beseech thee, O Lord.

From 'Salvator Mundi', 19th century

Dear God, be good to me;
the sea is so wide,
and my boat is so small.

A prayer used by Breton fishermen

O heavenly Father,
send into our hearts
and into the hearts of all people everywhere
the spirit of our Lord Jesus Christ.

John Oxenham, 1861-1941

O Lord,
help us to be the masters of ourselves
that we may be the servants of others.

Sir Alec Paterson, 1884-1947

Selections from the Psalter

PSALM 1

1 Happy are they who have not walked
   in the counsel of the wicked,
   nor lingered in the way of sinners,
   nor sat in the seats of the scornful!

2 Their delight is in the law of the Lord,
   and they meditate on his law day and night.

3 They are like trees planted by streams of water,
   bearing fruit in due season, with leaves that do not wither;
   everything they do shall prosper.

4 It is not so with the wicked;
   they are like chaff which the wind blows away.

5 Therefore the wicked shall not stand upright
   when judgment comes,
   nor the sinner in the council of the righteous.

6 For the Lord knows the way of the righteous,
   but the way of the wicked is doomed.

PSALM 2

1 Why are the nations in an uproar?
   Why do the peoples mutter empty threats?

2 Why do the kings of the earth rise up in revolt,
   and the princes plot together,
   against the Lord and against his anointed?

3 'Let us break their yoke', they say:
   'let us cast off their bonds from us'.

4   He whose throne is in heaven is laughing;
     the Lord has them in derision.

5   Then he speaks to them in his wrath,
     and his rage fills them with terror.

                    *   *   *

6   'I myself have set my king
     upon my holy hill of Zion.'

7   Let me announce the decree of the Lord:
     he said to me, 'You are my Son;
     this day have I begotten you.

8   Ask of me, and I will give you the nations
     for your inheritance
     and the ends of the earth for your possession.

9   You shall crush them with an iron rod
     and shatter them like a piece of pottery'.

10 And now, you kings, be wise;
     be warned, you rulers of the earth.

11 Submit to the Lord with fear,
     and with trembling bow before him;

     Lest he be angry and you perish;
     for his wrath is quickly kindled.

     Happy are they all
     who take refuge in him!

PSALM 3

1   Lord, how many adversaries I have!
     how many there are who rise up against me!

2 How many there are who say of me,
   'There is no help for him in his God'.

3 But you, O Lord, are a shield about me;
   you are my glory, the one who lifts up my head.

4 I call aloud upon the Lord,
   and he answers me from his holy hill;

5 I lie down and go to sleep;
   I wake again, because the Lord sustains me.

6 I do not fear the multitudes of people
   who set themselves against me all around.

7 Rise up, O Lord; set me free, O my God;
   surely, you will strike all my enemies across the face,
   you will break the teeth of the wicked.

8 Deliverance belongs to the Lord.
   Your blessing be upon your people!

PSALM 4

1 Answer me when I call, O God, defender of my cause;
   you set me free when I am hard-pressed;
   have mercy on me and hear my prayer.

2 'You mortals, how long will you dishonour my glory;
   how long will you worship dumb idols
   and run after false gods?'

3 Know that the Lord does wonders for the faithful;
   when I call upon the Lord, he will hear me.

4 Tremble, then, and do not sin;
   speak to your heart in silence upon your bed.

5   Offer the appointed sacrifices
     and put your trust in the Lord.

6   Many are saying,
     'Oh, that we might see better times!'
     Lift up the light of your countenance upon us, O Lord.

7   You have put gladness in my heart,
     more than when grain and wine and oil increase.

8   I lie down in peace; at once I fall asleep;
     for only you, Lord, make me dwell in safety.

PSALM 5:1-8

1   Give ear to my words, O Lord;
     consider my meditation.

2   Hearken to my cry for help, my King and my God,
     for I make my prayer to you.

3   In the morning, Lord, you hear my voice;
     early in the morning
     I make my appeal and watch for you.

4   For you are not a God who takes pleasure in wickedness,
     and evil cannot dwell with you.

5   The boastful cannot stand in your sight;
     you hate all those who work wickedness.

6   You destroy those who speak lies;
     the bloodthirsty and deceitful, O Lord, you abhor.

7   But as for me, through the greatness of your mercy
     I will go into your house;
     I will bow down toward your holy temple in awe of you.

8   Lead me, O Lord, in your righteousness,
     because of those who lie in wait for me;
     make your way straight before me.

PSALM 8

1 O Lord our ruler,
   how exalted is your name in all the world!

2 Out of the mouths of infants and children
   your majesty is praised above the heavens.

   You have set up a stronghold against your adversaries,
   to quell the enemy and the avenger.

3 When I consider your heavens, the work of your fingers,
   the moon and the stars you have set in their courses,

4 What is man that you should be mindful of him?
   the son of man that you should seek him out?

5 You have made him but little lower than the angels;
   you adorn him with glory and honour;

6 You give him mastery over the works of your hands;
   you put all things under his feet;

7 All sheep and oxen,
   even the wild beasts of the field,

8 The birds of the air, the fish of the sea,
   and whatsoever walks in the paths of the sea.

9 O Lord our ruler,
   how exalted is your name in all the world!

PSALM 9:11-20

11 Sing praise to the Lord who dwells in Zion;
   proclaim to the peoples the things he has done.

12 The avenger of blood will remember them;
   he will not forget the cry of the afflicted.

13 Have pity on me, O Lord;
 see the misery I suffer from those who hate me,
 O you who lift me up from the gate of death;

14 So that I may tell of all your praises
and rejoice in your salvation
 in the gates of the city of Zion.

15 The ungodly have fallen into the pit they dug,
 and in the snare they set is their own foot caught.

16 The Lord is known by his acts of justice;
 the wicked are trapped
 in the works of their own hands.

17 The wicked shall be given over to the grave,
 and also all the peoples that forget God.

18 For the needy shall not always be forgotten,
 and the hope of the poor shall not perish for ever.

19 Rise up, O Lord, let not the ungodly have the upper hand;
 let them be judged before you.

20 Put fear in them, O Lord;
 let the ungodly know they are but mortal.

PSALM 10:12-18

12 Rise up, O Lord;
lift up your hand, O God;
 do not forget the afflicted.

13 Why should the wicked revile God?
 why should they say in their heart, 'You do not care?'

14 Surely, you behold trouble and misery;
    you see it and take it into your own hand.

    The helpless commit themselves to you,
    for you are the helper of orphans.

15 Break the power of the wicked and evil;
    search out their wickedness until you find none.

16 The Lord is king for ever and ever;
    the ungodly shall perish from his land.

17 The Lord will hear the desire of the humble;
    you will strengthen their heart
    and your ears shall hear;

18 To give justice to the orphan and oppressed,
    so that mere mortals may strike terror no more.

PSALM 13

1 How long, O Lord?
    will you forget me for ever?
    how long will you hide your face from me?

2 How long shall I have perplexity in my mind,
    and grief in my heart, day after day?
    how long shall my enemy triumph over me?

3 Look upon me and answer me, O Lord my God;
    give light to my eyes, lest I sleep in death;

4 Lest my enemy say, 'I have prevailed over him'
    and my foes rejoice that I have fallen.

5 But I put my trust in your mercy;
    my heart is joyful because of your saving help.

6 I will sing to the Lord, for he has dealt with me richly;
    I will praise the name of the Lord Most High.

PSALM 14

1 The fool has said in his heart, 'There is no God'.
   All are corrupt and commit abominable acts;
   there is none who does any good.

2 The Lord looks down from heaven upon us all,
   to see if there is any who is wise,
   if there is one who seeks after God.

3 Every one has proved faithless;
   all alike have turned bad;
   there is none who does good; no, not one.

4 Have they no knowledge, all those evildoers
   who eat up my people like bread
   and do not call upon the Lord?

5 See how they tremble with fear,
   because God is in the company of the righteous.

6 Their aim is to confound the plans of the afflicted,
   but the Lord is their refuge.

7 Oh, that Israel's deliverance would come out of Zion!
   when the Lord restores the fortunes of his people,
   Jacob will rejoice and Israel be glad.

PSALM 15

1 Lord, who may dwell in your tabernacle?
   who may abide upon your holy hill?

2 Whoever leads a blameless life and does what is right,
   who speaks the truth from his heart.

3   There is no guile upon his tongue;
    he does no evil to his friend;
      he does not heap contempt upon his neighbour.

4   In his sight the wicked is rejected,
      but he honours those who fear the Lord.

    He has sworn to do no wrong
      and does not take back his word.

5   He does not give his money in hope of gain,
      nor does he take a bribe against the innocent.

    Whoever does these things
      shall never be overthrown.

PSALM 16

1   Protect me, O God, for I take refuge in you;
2   **I have said to the Lord, 'You are my Lord,**
      my good above all other'.

3   All my delight is upon the godly that are in the land,
      upon those who are noble among the people.

4   But those who run after other gods
      shall have their troubles multiplied.

    Their libations of blood I will not offer,
      nor take the names of their gods upon my lips.

          *   *   *

5   O Lord, you are my portion and my cup;
      it is you who uphold my lot.

6   My boundaries enclose a pleasant land;
      indeed, I have a goodly heritage.

7   I will bless the Lord who gives me counsel;
       my heart teaches me, night after night.

8   I have set the Lord always before me;
       because he is at my right hand I shall not fall.

9   My heart, therefore, is glad, and my spirit rejoices;
       my body also shall rest in hope.

10   For you will not abandon me to the grave,
       nor let your holy one see the Pit.

11   You will show me the path of life;
       in your presence there is fullness of joy,
       and in your right hand are pleasures for evermore.

PSALM 17:1-7

1   Hear my plea of innocence, O Lord;
     give heed to my cry;
       listen to my prayer,
       which does not come from lying lips.

2   Let my vindication come forth from your presence;
       let your eyes be fixed on justice.

3   Weigh my heart, summon me by night,
       melt me down; you will find no impurity in me.

4   I give no offence with my mouth as others do;
       I have heeded the words of your lips.

5   My footsteps hold fast to the ways of your law;
       in your paths my feet shall not stumble.

6   I call upon you, O God, for you will answer me;
       incline your ear to me and hear my words.

7   Show me your marvellous loving-kindness,
       O Saviour of those who take refuge at your right hand
       from those who rise up against them.

PSALM 19

1   The heavens declare the glory of God,
    and the firmament shows his handiwork.

2   One day tells its tale to another,
    and one night imparts knowledge to another.

3   Although they have no words or language,
    and their voices are not heard,

4   Their sound has gone out into all lands,
    and their message to the ends of the world.

    In the deep has he set a pavilion for the sun;
5   **it comes forth like a bridegroom out of his chamber;**
    it rejoices like a champion to run its course.

6   It goes forth from the uttermost edge of the heavens
    and runs about to the end of it again;
    nothing is hidden from its burning heat.

              *   *   *

7   The law of the Lord is perfect and revives the soul;
    the testimony of the Lord is sure
    and gives wisdom to the innocent.

8   The statutes of the Lord are just and rejoice the heart;
    the commandment of the Lord is clear
    and gives light to the eyes.

9   The fear of the Lord is clean and endures for ever;
    the judgments of the Lord are true
    and righteous altogether.

10 More to be desired are they than gold,
    more than much fine gold,
    sweeter far than honey, than honey in the comb.

11   By them also is your servant enlightened,
    and in keeping them there is great reward.

12   Who can tell how often he offends?
    cleanse me from my secret faults.

13   Above all, keep your servant from presumptuous sins;
    let them not get dominion over me;
    then shall I be whole and sound,
    and innocent of a great offence.

14   Let the words of my mouth and the meditation of my heart
    be acceptable in your sight,
    O Lord, my strength and my redeemer.

PSALM 20

1   May the Lord answer you in the day of trouble,
    the name of the God of Jacob defend you;

2   Send you help from his holy place
    and strengthen you out of Zion;

3   Remember all your offerings
    and accept your burnt sacrifice;

4   Grant you your heart's desire
    and prosper all your plans.

5   We will shout for joy at your victory
    and triumph in the name of our God;
    may the Lord grant all your requests.

6   Now I know that the Lord gives victory to his anointed;
    he will answer him out of his holy heaven,
    with the victorious strength of his right hand.

7   Some put their trust in chariots and some in horses,
       but we will call upon the name of the Lord our God.

8   They collapse and fall down,
       but we will arise and stand upright.

9   O Lord, give victory to the king
       and answer us when we call.

PSALM 21:1-7

1   The king rejoices in your strength, O Lord;
       how greatly he exults in your victory!

2   You have given him his heart's desire;
       you have not denied him the request of his lips.

3   For you meet him with blessings of prosperity,
       and set a crown of fine gold upon his head.

4   He asked you for life, and you gave it to him;
       length of days, for ever and ever.

5   His honour is great, because of your victory;
       splendour and majesty have you bestowed upon him.

6   For you will give him everlasting felicity
       and will make him glad with the joy of your presence.

7   For the king puts his trust in the Lord;
       **because of the loving-kindness of the Most High,
       he will not fall.**

PSALM 22:1-18, 25-31

1 My God, my God, why have you forsaken me?
   and are so far from my cry
   and from the words of my distress?

2 O my God, I cry in the daytime, but you do not answer;
   by night as well, but I find no rest.

3 Yet you are the Holy One,
   enthroned upon the praises of Israel.

4 Our forebears put their trust in you;
   they trusted, and you delivered them.

5 They cried out to you and were delivered;
   they trusted in you and were not put to shame.

6 But as for me, I am a worm and no man,
   scorned by all and despised by the people.

7 All who see me laugh me to scorn;
   they curl their lips and wag their heads, saying,

8 'He trusted in the Lord; let him deliver him;
   let him rescue him, if he delights in him'.

9 Yet you are the one who took me out of the womb,
   and kept me safe upon my mother's breast.

10 I have been entrusted to you ever since I was born;
   you were my God
   when I was still in my mother's womb.

11 Be not far from me, for trouble is near,
   and there is none to help.

12 Many young bulls encircle me;
   strong bulls of Bashan surround me.

13 They open wide their jaws at me,
   like a ravening and a roaring lion.

14 I am poured out like water;
   all my bones are out of joint;
      my heart within my breast is melting wax.

15 My mouth is dried out like a pot-sherd;
   my tongue sticks to the roof of my mouth;
      and you have laid me in the dust of the grave.

16 Packs of dogs close me in,
   and gangs of evildoers circle around me;
      they pierce my hands and my feet;
17   **I can count all my bones.**

   They stare and gloat over me;
18   **they divide my garments among them;**
      they cast lots for my clothing.

*   *   *

25 My praise is of him in the great assembly;
      I will perform my vows
      in the presence of those who worship him.

26 The poor shall eat and be satisfied,
   and those who seek the Lord shall praise him:
      'May your heart live for ever!'

27 All the ends of the earth shall remember
   and turn to the Lord,
      and all the families of the nations
      shall bow before him.

28 For kingship belongs to the Lord;
      he rules over the nations.

29 To him alone all who sleep in the earth
   bow down in worship;
      all who go down to the dust fall before him.

30 My soul shall live for him;
my descendants shall serve him;
they shall be known as the Lord's for ever.

31 They shall come and make known to a people yet unborn
the saving deeds that he has done.

PSALM 23

1 The Lord is my shepherd;
I shall not be in want.

2 He makes me lie down in green pastures
and leads me beside still waters.

3 He revives my soul
**and guides me along right pathways
for his name's sake.**

4 Though I walk through the valley of the shadow of death,
I shall fear no evil;
**for you are with me;
your rod and your staff, they comfort me.**

5 You spread a table before me
in the presence of those who trouble me;
**you have anointed my head with oil,
and my cup is running over.**

6 Surely your goodness and mercy shall follow me
all the days of my life,
and I will dwell in the house of the Lord for ever.

PSALM 24

1 The earth is the Lord's and all that is in it,
  the world and all who dwell therein.

2 For it is he who founded it upon the seas
  and made it firm upon the rivers of the deep.

3 'Who can ascend the hill of the Lord?
  and who can stand in his holy place?'

4 'Those who have clean hands and a pure heart,
  who have not pledged themselves to falsehood,
  nor sworn by what is a fraud.

5 They shall receive a blessing from the Lord
  and a just reward from the God of their salvation.'

6 Such is the generation of those who seek him,
  of those who seek your face, O God of Jacob.

7 Lift up your heads, O gates;
  lift them high, O everlasting doors;
  and the King of glory shall come in.

8 'Who is this King of glory?'
  'The Lord, strong and mighty,
  the Lord, mighty in battle.'

9 Lift up your heads, O gates;
  lift them high, O everlasting doors;
  and the King of glory shall come in.

10 'Who is he, this King of glory?'
  'The Lord of hosts,
  he is the King of glory.'

PSALM 25:1-10

1 To you, O Lord, I lift up my soul;
2 my God, I put my trust in you;
   let me not be humiliated,
   nor let my enemies triumph over me.

3 Let none who look to you be put to shame;
   let the treacherous be disappointed in their schemes.

4 Show me your ways, O Lord,
   and teach me your paths.

5 Lead me in your truth and teach me,
   for you are the God of my salvation;
   in you have I trusted all the day long.

6 Remember, O Lord, your compassion and love,
   for they are from everlasting.

7 Remember not the sins of my youth and my transgressions;
   remember me according to your love
   and for the sake of your goodness, O Lord.

8 Gracious and upright is the Lord;
   therefore he teaches sinners in his way.

9 He guides the humble in doing right
   and teaches his way to the lowly.

10 All the paths of the Lord are love and faithfulness
   to those who keep his covenant and his testimonies.

PSALM 26

1   Give judgment for me, O Lord,
     for I have lived with integrity;
       I have trusted in the Lord and have not faltered.

2   Test me, O Lord, and try me;
       examine my heart and my mind.

3   For your love is before my eyes;
       I have walked faithfully with you.

4   I have not sat with the worthless,
       nor do I consort with the deceitful.

5   I have hated the company of evildoers;
       I will not sit down with the wicked.

6   I will wash my hands in innocence, O Lord,
       that I may go in procession round your altar,

7   Singing aloud a song of thanksgiving,
       and recounting all your wonderful deeds.

8   Lord, I love the house in which you dwell
       and the place where your glory abides.

9   Do not sweep me away with sinners,
       nor my life with those who thirst for blood,

10 Whose hands are full of evil plots,
       and their right hand full of bribes.

11 As for me, I will live with integrity;
       redeem me, O Lord, and have pity on me.

12 My foot stands on level ground;
       in the full assembly I will bless the Lord.

PSALM 27

1   The Lord is my light and my salvation;
     whom then shall I fear?
          the Lord is the strength of my life;
          of whom then shall I be afraid?

2   When evildoers came upon me to eat up my flesh,
          it was they, my foes and my adversaries,
          who stumbled and fell.

3   Though an army should encamp against me,
          yet my heart shall not be afraid;

     And though war should rise up against me,
          yet will I put my trust in him.

4   One thing have I asked of the Lord;
     one thing I seek;
          that I may dwell in the house of the Lord
          all the days of my life;

     To behold the fair beauty of the Lord
          and to seek him in his temple.

5   For in the day of trouble
     he shall keep me safe in his shelter;
          he shall hide me in the secrecy of his dwelling
          and set me high upon a rock.

6   Even now he lifts up my head
          above my enemies round about me.

     Therefore I will offer in his dwelling an oblation
     with sounds of great gladness;
          I will sing and make music to the Lord.

*   *   *

7 Hearken to my voice, O Lord, when I call;
   have mercy on me and answer me.

8 You speak in my heart and say, 'Seek my face'.
   Your face, Lord, will I seek.

9 Hide not your face from me,
   nor turn away your servant in displeasure.

   You have been my helper:
   cast me not away;
   do not forsake me, O God of my salvation.

10 Though my father and my mother forsake me,
    the Lord will sustain me.

11 Show me your way, O Lord;
    lead me on a level path, because of my enemies.

12 Deliver me not into the hands of my adversaries,
    for false witnesses have risen up against me,
    and also those who speak malice.

13 What if I had not believed
    that I should see the goodness of the Lord
    in the land of the living!

14 O wait for the Lord's pleasure;
    be strong, and he shall comfort your heart;
    wait patiently for the Lord.

PSALM 28

1 O Lord, I call to you;
   my rock, do not be deaf to my cry;
   lest, if you do not hear me,
   I become like those who go down to the Pit.

2   Hear the voice of my prayer when I cry out to you,
    when I lift up my hands to your holy of holies.

3   Do not snatch me away with the wicked
    or with the evildoers,
    who speak peaceably with their neighbours,
    while strife is in their hearts.

4   Repay them according to their deeds,
    and according to the wickedness of their actions.

    According to the work of their hands repay them,
    and give them their just deserts.

5   They have no understanding of the Lord's doings,
    nor of the works of his hands;
    therefore he will break them down
    and not build them up.

6   Blessed is the Lord!
    for he has heard the voice of my prayer.

7   The Lord is my strength and my shield;
    my heart trusts in him, and I have been helped;

    Therefore my heart dances for joy,
    and in my song will I praise him.

8   The Lord is the strength of his people,
    a safe refuge for his anointed.

9   Save your people and bless your inheritance;
    shepherd them and carry them for ever.

PSALM 29

1   Ascribe to the Lord, you gods,
    ascribe to the Lord glory and strength.

2   Ascribe to the Lord the glory due to his name;
    worship the Lord in the beauty of holiness.

3 The voice of the Lord is upon the waters;
the God of glory thunders;
the Lord is upon the mighty waters.

4 The voice of the Lord is a powerful voice;
the voice of the Lord is a voice of splendour.

5 The voice of the Lord breaks the cedar trees;
the Lord breaks the cedars of Lebanon;

6 He makes Lebanon skip like a calf,
and Mount Hermon like a young wild ox.

7 The voice of the Lord splits the flames of fire;
8 the voice of the Lord shakes the wilderness;
the Lord shakes the wilderness of Kadesh.

9 The voice of the Lord makes the oak trees writhe
and strips the forests bare.

And in the temple of the Lord
all are crying, 'Glory!'

10 The Lord sits enthroned above the flood;
the Lord sits enthroned as king for evermore.

11 The Lord shall give strength to his people;
the Lord shall give his people the blessing of peace.

PSALM 30

1 I will exalt you, O Lord,
because you have lifted me up
and have not let my enemies triumph over me.

2 O Lord my God, I cried out to you,
and you restored me to health.

3 You brought me up, O Lord, from the dead;
you restored my life as I was going down to the grave.

*   *   *

4   Sing to the Lord, you servants of his;
    give thanks for the remembrance of his holiness.

5   For his wrath endures but the twinkling of an eye,
    his favour for a lifetime.

    Weeping may spend the night
    but joy comes in the morning.

6   While I felt secure, I said,
    'I shall never be disturbed.

7   **You, Lord, with your favour,**
    made me as strong as the mountains'.

    Then you hid your face,
    and I was filled with fear.

8   I cried to you, O Lord;
    I pleaded with the Lord, saying,

9   'What profit is there in my blood,
    if I go down to the Pit?
    will the dust praise you
    or declare your faithfulness?

10 Hear, O Lord, and have mercy upon me;
    O Lord, be my helper'.

11 You have turned my wailing into dancing;
    you have put off my sack-cloth
    and clothed me with joy.

12 Therefore my heart sings to you without ceasing;
    O Lord my God, I will give you thanks for ever.

PSALM 31:1-16

1   In you, O Lord, have I taken refuge;
    let me never be put to shame;
    deliver me in your righteousness.

2 Incline your ear to me;
    make haste to deliver me.

Be my strong rock, a castle to keep me safe,
3 for you are my crag and my stronghold;
    for the sake of your name, lead me and guide me.

4 Take me out of the net that they have secretly set for me,
    for you are my tower of strength.

5 Into your hands I commend my spirit,
    for you have redeemed me,
    O Lord, O God of truth.

6 I hate those who cling to worthless idols,
    and I put my trust in the Lord.

7 I will rejoice and be glad because of your mercy;
    for you have seen my affliction;
    you know my distress.

8 You have not shut me up in the power of the enemy;
    you have set my feet in an open place.

       *   *   *

9 Have mercy on me, O Lord, for I am in trouble;
    my eye is consumed with sorrow,
    and also my throat and my belly.

10 For my life is wasted with grief,
    and my years with sighing;
    my strength fails me because of affliction,
    and my bones are consumed.

11 I have become a reproach to all my enemies
    and even to my neighbours,
    a dismay to those of my acquaintance;
    when they see me in the street they avoid me.

12   I am forgotten like a dead man, out of mind;
        I am as useless as a broken pot.

13   For I have heard the whispering of the crowd;
        fear is all around;
          they put their heads together against me;
          they plot to take my life.

14   But as for me, I have trusted in you, O Lord.
        I have said, 'You are my God.

15   My times are in your hand;
        rescue me from the hand of my enemies,
        and from those who persecute me.

16   Make your face to shine upon your servant,
        and in your loving-kindness save me'.

PSALM 32

1   Happy are they whose transgressions are forgiven,
        and whose sin is put away!

2   Happy are they to whom the Lord imputes no guilt,
        and in whose spirit there is no guile!

3   While I held my tongue, my bones withered away,
        because of my groaning all day long.

4   For your hand was heavy upon me day and night;
        my moisture was dried up as in the heat of summer.

5   Then I acknowledged my sin to you,
        and did not conceal my guilt.

     I said, 'I will confess my transgressions to the Lord'.
        Then you forgave me the guilt of my sin.

6 Therefore all the faithful will make their prayers to you
in time of trouble;
   when the great waters overflow,
   they shall not reach them.

7 You are my hiding-place;
you preserve me from trouble;
   you surround me with shouts of deliverance.

8 'I will instruct you and teach you
in the way that you should go;
   I will guide you with my eye.

9 Do not be like horse or mule,
which have no understanding;
   who must be fitted with bit and bridle,
   or else they will not stay near you.'

10 Great are the tribulations of the wicked;
   but mercy embraces those who trust in the Lord.

11 Be glad, you righteous, and rejoice in the Lord;
   shout for joy, all who are true of heart.

PSALM 33

1 Rejoice in the Lord, you righteous;
   it is good for the just to sing praises.

2 Praise the Lord with the harp;
   play to him on the psaltery and lyre.

3 Sing for him a new song;
   sound a fanfare with all your skill upon the trumpet.

4 For the word of the Lord is right,
   and all his works are sure.

5   He loves righteousness and justice;
      the loving-kindness of the Lord fills the whole earth.

6   By the word of the Lord were the heavens made,
      by the breath of his mouth all the heavenly hosts.

7   He gathers up the waters of the ocean as in a water-skin
      and stores up the depths of the sea.

8   Let the whole earth fear the Lord;
      let all who dwell in the world stand in awe of him.

9   For he spoke, and it came to pass;
      he commanded, and it stood fast.

10 The Lord brings the will of the nations to naught;
      he thwarts the designs of the peoples.

11 But the Lord's will stands fast for ever,
      and the designs of his heart from age to age.

                    *   *   *

12 Happy is the nation whose God is the Lord!
      happy the people he has chosen to be his own!

13 The Lord looks down from heaven,
      and beholds all the people in the world.

14 From where he sits enthroned he turns his gaze
      on all who dwell on the earth.

15 He fashions all the hearts of them
      and understands all their works.

16 There is no king that can be saved by a mighty army;
      a strong man is not delivered by his great strength.

17 The horse is a vain hope for deliverance;
      for all its strength it cannot save.

18   Behold, the eye of the Lord is upon those who fear him,
      on those who wait upon his love.

19   To pluck their lives from death,
      and to feed them in time of famine.

20   Our soul waits for the Lord;
      he is our help and our shield.

21   Indeed, our heart rejoices in him,
      for in his holy name we put our trust.

22   Let your loving-kindness, O Lord, be upon us,
      as we have put our trust in you.

PSALM 34

1   I will bless the Lord at all times;
      his praise shall ever be in my mouth.

2   I will glory in the Lord;
      let the humble hear and rejoice.

3   Proclaim with me the greatness of the Lord;
      let us exalt his name together.

4   I sought the Lord, and he answered me
      and delivered me out of all my terror.

5   Look upon him and be radiant,
      and let not your faces be ashamed.

6   I called in my affliction and the Lord heard me
      and saved me from all my troubles.

7   The angel of the Lord encompasses those who fear him,
      and he will deliver them.

8   Taste and see that the Lord is good;
      happy are they who trust in him!

9 Fear the Lord, you that are his saints,
  for those who fear him lack nothing.

10 The young lions lack and suffer hunger,
  **but those who seek the Lord
  lack nothing that is good.**

*   *   *

11 Come, children, and listen to me;
  I will teach you the fear of the Lord.

12 Who among you loves life
  and desires long life to enjoy prosperity?

13 Keep your tongue from evil-speaking
  and your lips from lying words.

14 Turn from evil and do good;
  seek peace and pursue it.

15 The eyes of the Lord are upon the righteous,
  and his ears are open to their cry.

16 The face of the Lord is against those who do evil,
  to root out the remembrance of them from the earth.

17 The righteous cry, and the Lord hears them
  and delivers them from all their troubles.

18 The Lord is near to the brokenhearted
  and will save those whose spirits are crushed.

19 Many are the troubles of the righteous,
  but the Lord will deliver him out of them all.

20 He will keep safe all his bones;
  not one of them shall be broken.

21 Evil shall slay the wicked,
  and those who hate the righteous will be punished.

22 The Lord ransoms the life of his servants,
  and none will be punished who trust in him.

PSALM 35:17-28

17   O Lord, how long will you look on?
      rescue me from the roaring beasts,
      and my life from the young lions.

18   I will give you thanks in the great congregation;
      I will praise you in the mighty throng.

19   Do not let my treacherous foes rejoice over me,
      nor let those who hate me without a cause
      wink at each other.

20   For they do not plan for peace,
      but invent deceitful schemes
      against the quiet in the land.

21   They opened their mouths at me and said,
      'Aha! we saw it with our own eyes'.

22   You saw it, O Lord; do not be silent;
      O Lord, be not far from me.

23   Awake, arise, to my cause!
      to my defence, my God and my Lord!

24   Give me justice, O Lord my God,
      according to your righteousness;
      do not let them triumph over me.

25   Do not let them say in their hearts,
      'Aha! just what we want!'
      Do not let them say, 'We have swallowed him up'.

26   Let all who rejoice at my ruin be ashamed and disgraced;
      let those who boast against me
      be clothed with dismay and shame.

27   Let those who favour my cause
    sing out with joy and be glad;
      let them say always, 'Great is the Lord,
      who desires the prosperity of his servant'.

28   And my tongue shall be talking of your righteousness
      and of your praise all the day long.

PSALM 36:5-10

5   Your love, O Lord, reaches to the heavens,
      and your faithfulness to the clouds.

6   Your righteousness is like the strong mountains,
      your justice like the great deep;
      you save both man and beast, O Lord.

7   How priceless is your love, O God!
      your people take refuge
      under the shadow of your wings.

8   They feast upon the abundance of your house;
      you give them drink from the river of your delights.

9   For with you is the well of life,
      and in your light we see light.

10   Continue your loving-kindness to those who know you,
      and your favour to those who are true of heart.

PSALM 37:1-11

1   Do not fret yourself because of evil-doers;
      do not be jealous of those who do wrong.

2   For they shall soon wither like the grass,
      and like the green grass fade away.

3   Put your trust in the Lord and do good;
       dwell in the land and feed on its riches.

4   Take delight in the Lord,
       and he shall give you your heart's desire.

5   Commit your way to the Lord and put your trust in him,
       and he will bring it to pass.

6   He will make your righteousness as clear as the light
       and your just dealing as the noonday.

7   Be still before the Lord
       and wait patiently for him.

       Do not fret yourself over the one who prospers,
       the one who succeeds in evil schemes.

8   Refrain from anger, leave rage alone;
       do not fret yourself; it leads only to evil.

9   For evildoers shall be cut off,
       but those who wait upon the Lord
       shall possess the land.

10   In a little while the wicked shall be no more;
       you shall search out their place,
       but they will not be there.

11   But the lowly shall possess the land;
       they will delight in abundance of peace.

PSALM 40:1-11

1   I waited patiently for the Lord;
       he stooped to me and heard my cry.

2 He lifted me out of the desolate pit,
out of the mire and clay;
he set my feet upon a high cliff
and made my footing sure.

3 He put a new song in my mouth,
a song of praise to our God;
many shall see, and stand in awe,
and put their trust in the Lord.

4 Happy are they who trust in the Lord!
they do not resort to evil spirits or turn to false gods.

5 Great things are they that you have done, O Lord my God!
how great your wonders and your plans for us!
there is none who can be compared with you.

*   *   *

6 In sacrifice and offering you take no pleasure
(you have given me ears to hear you);

7 Burnt-offering and sin-offering you have not required,
and so I said, 'Behold I come.

8 In the roll of the book it is written concerning me:
I love to do your will, O my God;
your law is deep in my heart '.

9 I proclaimed righteousness in the great congregation;
behold, I did not restrain my lips;
and that, O Lord, you know.

10 Your righteousness have I not hidden in my heart;
I have spoken of your faithfulness and your deliverance;
I have not concealed your love and faithfulness
from the great congregation.

11 You are the Lord;
do not withhold your compassion from me;
let your love and your faithfulness
keep me safe for ever.

PSALM 41

1 Happy are they who consider the poor and needy!
   the Lord will deliver them in the time of trouble.

2 The Lord preserves them and keeps them alive,
   so that they may be happy in the land;
   he does not hand them over
   to the will of their enemies.

3 The Lord sustains them on their sickbed
   and ministers to them in their illness.

4 I said, 'Lord, be merciful to me;
   heal me, for I have sinned against you'.

5 My enemies are saying wicked things about me:
   'When will he die, and his name perish?'

6 Even if they come to see me, they speak empty words;
   their heart collects false rumours;
   they go outside and spread them.

7 All my enemies whisper together about me
   and devise evil against me.

8 'A deadly thing', they say, 'has fastened on him;
   he has taken to his bed and will never get up again'.

9 Even my best friend, whom I trusted,
   who broke bread with me,
   has lifted up his heel and turned against me.

10 But you, O Lord, be merciful to me and raise me up,
    and I shall repay them.

11 By this I know you are pleased with me,
    that my enemy does not triumph over me.

12 In my integrity you hold me fast,
   and shall set me before your face for ever.

13 Blessed be the Lord God of Israel,
   from age to age. Amen. Amen.

PSALM 42

1 As the deer longs for the water-brooks,
  so longs my soul for you, O God.

2 My soul is athirst for God, athirst for the living God;
  when shall I come to appear
  before the presence of God?

3 My tears have been my food day and night,
  while all day long they say to me,
  'Where now is your God?'

4 I pour out my soul when I think on these things:
  how I went with the multitude
  and led them into the house of God,

  With the voice of praise and thanksgiving,
  among those who keep holy-day.

5 Why are you so full of heaviness, O my soul?
  and why are you disquieted within me?

  Put your trust in God;
  for I will yet give thanks to him,
  who is the help of my countenance, and my God.

6 My soul is heavy within me;
  therefore I will remember you
  from the land of Jordan,
  and from the peak of Mizar
  among the heights of Hermon.

7   One deep calls to another in the noise of your cataracts;
all your rapids and floods have gone over me.

8   The Lord grants his loving-kindness in the daytime;
in the night season his song is with me,
a prayer to the God of my life.

9   I will say to the God of my strength,
'Why have you forgotten me?
and why do I go so heavily
while the enemy oppresses me?'

10   While my bones are being broken,
my enemies mock me to my face;

All day long they mock me
and say to me, 'Where now is your God?'

11   Why are you so full of heaviness, O my soul?
and why are you so disquieted within me?
Put your trust in God;
for I will yet give thanks to him,
who is the help of my countenance, and my God.

PSALM 43

1   Give judgment for me, O God,
and defend my cause against an ungodly people;
deliver me from the deceitful and the wicked.

2   For you are the God of my strength;
why have you put me from you?
and why do I go so heavily
while the enemy oppresses me?

3   Send out your light and your truth, that they may lead me,
and bring me to your holy hill and to your dwelling;

4   That I may go to the altar of God,
to the God of my joy and gladness;
and on the harp I will give thanks to you,
O God my God.

5   Why are you so full of heaviness, O my soul?
      and why are you so disquieted within me?

Put your trust in God;
      for I will yet give thanks to him,
      who is the help of my countenance, and my God.

PSALM 44:1-8

1   We have heard with our ears, O God,
our forebears have told us,
      the deeds you did in their days, in the days of old.

2   How with your hand you drove the peoples out
and planted our forebears in the land;
      how you destroyed nations
      and made your people flourish.

3   For they did not take the land by their sword,
nor did their arm win the victory for them;
      but your right hand, your arm,
      and the light of your countenance,
      because you favoured them.

4   You are my King and my God;
      you command victories for Jacob.

5   Through you we pushed back our adversaries;
      through your name we trampled
      on those who rose up against us.

6   For I do not rely on my bow,
      and my sword does not give me the victory.

7   Surely, you gave us victory over our adversaries
      and put those who hate us to shame.

8   Every day we gloried in God,
      and we will praise your name for ever.

PSALM 45

1 My heart is stirring with a noble song;
  let me recite what I have fashioned for the king;
    my tongue shall be the pen of a skilled writer.

2 You are the fairest of men;
    grace flows from your lips,
    because God has blessed you for ever.

3 Strap your sword upon your thigh, O mighty warrior,
    in your pride and in your majesty.

4 Ride out and conquer in the cause of truth
    and for the sake of justice.

5 Your right hand will show you marvellous things;
    your arrows are very sharp, O mighty warrior.

  The peoples are falling at your feet,
    and the king's enemies are losing heart.

6 Your throne, O God, endures for ever and ever,
    a sceptre of righteousness
    is the sceptre of your kingdom;
7   **you love righteousness and hate iniquity.**

  Therefore God, your God, has anointed you
    with the oil of gladness above your fellows.

8 All your garments are fragrant with myrrh, aloes, and cassia,
    and the music of strings from ivory palaces
    makes you glad.

9 Kings' daughters stand among the ladies of the court;
    on your right hand is the queen,
    adorned with the gold of Ophir.

10   'Hear, O daughter; consider and listen closely;
      forget your people and your father's house.

11   The king will have pleasure in your beauty;
      he is your master; therefore do him honour.

12   The people of Tyre are here with a gift;
      the rich among the people seek your favour.'

13   All glorious is the princess as she enters;
      her gown is cloth-of-gold.

14   In embroidered apparel she is brought to the king;
      after her the bridesmaids follow in procession.

15   With joy and gladness they are brought,
      and enter into the palace of the king.

16   'In place of fathers, O king, you shall have sons;
      you shall make them princes over all the earth.

17   I will make your name to be remembered
    from one generation to another;
      therefore nations will praise you for ever and ever.'

PSALM 46

1   God is our refuge and strength,
      a very present help in trouble.

2   Therefore we will not fear, though the earth be moved,
      and though the mountains be toppled
      into the depths of the sea;

3   Though its waters rage and foam,
      and though the mountains tremble at its tumult.

    The Lord of hosts is with us;
      the God of Jacob is our stronghold.

4   There is a river whose streams make glad the city of God,
      the holy habitations of the Most High.

5   God is in the midst of her;
     she shall not be overthrown;
        God shall help her at the break of day.

6   The nations make much ado, and the kingdoms are shaken;
        God has spoken, and the earth shall melt away.

7   The Lord of hosts is with us;
        the God of Jacob is our stronghold.

8   Come now and look upon the works of the Lord,
        what awesome things he has done on earth.

9   It is he who makes war to cease in all the world;
        he breaks the bow, and shatters the spear,
        and burns the shields with fire.

10   'Be still, then, and know that I am God;
        I will be exalted among the nations;
        I will be exalted in the earth.'

11   The Lord of hosts is with us;
        the God of Jacob is our stronghold.

PSALM 47

1   Clap your hands, all you peoples;
        shout to God with a cry of joy.

2   For the Lord Most High is to be feared;
        he is the great king over all the earth.

3   He subdues the people under us,
        and the nations under our feet.

4   He chooses our inheritance for us
        the pride of Jacob whom he loves.

5   God has gone up with a shout,
        the Lord with the sound of the ram's-horn.

6   Sing praises to God, sing praises;
       sing praises to our king, sing praises.

7   For God is king of all the earth;
       sing praises with all your skill.

8   God reigns over the nations;
       God sits upon his holy throne.

9   The nobles of the peoples have gathered together
       with the people of the God of Abraham.

10   The rulers of the earth belong to God,
       and he is highly exalted.

PSALM 48

1   Great is the Lord, and highly to be praised;
       in the city of our God is his holy hill.

2   Beautiful and lofty, the joy of all the earth,
       is the hill of Zion,
       the very centre of the world
       and the city of the great king.

3   God is in her citadels;
       he is known to be her sure refuge.

4   Behold, the kings of the earth assembled
       and marched forward together.

5   They looked and were astounded;
       they retreated and fled in terror.

6   Trembling seized them there;
       they writhed like a woman in childbirth,

7   **like ships of the sea**
       when the east wind shatters them.

8   As we have heard, so have we seen,
     in the city of the Lord of hosts, in the city of our God;
        God has established her for ever.

9   We have waited in silence
     on your loving-kindness, O God,
        in the midst of your temple.

10   Your praise, like your name, O God,
     reaches to the world's end;
        your right hand is full of justice.

11   Let Mount Zion be glad
     and the cities of Judah rejoice,
        because of your judgments.

12   Make the circuit of Zion;
     walk round about her;
        count the number of her towers.

13   Consider well her bulwarks;
     examine her strongholds;
        that you may tell those who come after.

14   This God is our God for ever and ever;
        he shall be our guide for evermore.

PSALM 50:1-15

1   The Lord, the God of gods, has spoken;
        **he has called the earth from the rising of the sun
        to its setting.**

2   Out of Zion, perfect in its beauty,
        God reveals himself in glory.

3 Our God will come and will not keep silence;
   before him there is a consuming flame,
   and round about him a raging storm.

4 He calls the heavens and the earth from above
   to witness the judgment of his people.

5 'Gather before me my loyal followers,
   those who have made a covenant with me
   and sealed it with sacrifice.'

6 Let the heavens declare the rightness of his cause;
   for God himself is judge.

      *   *   *

7 Hear, my people, and I will speak:
   'O Israel, I will bear witness against you;
   for I am God, your God.

8 I do not accuse you because of your sacrifices;
   your offerings are always before me.

9 I will take no bull-calf from your stalls,
   nor he-goats out of your pens;

10 For the beasts of the forest are mine,
   the herds in their thousands upon the hills.

11 I know every bird in the sky,
   and the creatures of the fields are in my sight.

12 If I were hungry, I would not tell you,
   for the whole world is mine and all that is in it.

13 Do you think I eat the flesh of bulls,
   or drink the blood of goats?

14 Offer to God a sacrifice of thanksgiving
   and make good your vows to the Most High.

15 Call upon me in the day of trouble;
   I will deliver you, and you shall honour me'.

PSALM 51:1-17

1 Have mercy on me, O God,
   according to your loving-kindness;
     in your great compassion blot out my offences.

2 Wash me through and through from my wickedness
     and cleanse me from my sin.

3 For I know my transgressions,
     and my sin is ever before me.

4 Against you only have I sinned
     and done what is evil in your sight.

   And so you are justified when you speak
     and upright in your judgment.

5 Indeed, I have been wicked from my birth,
     a sinner from my mother's womb.

6 For behold, you look for truth deep within me,
     and will make me understand wisdom secretly.

7 Purge me from sin, and I shall be pure;
     wash me, and I shall be clean indeed.

8 Make me hear of joy and gladness,
     that the body you have broken may rejoice.

9 Hide your face from my sins
     and blot out all my iniquities.

  *   *   *

10 Create in me a clean heart, O God,
     and renew a right spirit within me.

11 Cast me not away from your presence
     and take not your holy Spirit from me.

12 Give me the joy of your saving help again,
   and sustain me with your bountiful Spirit.

                    *   *   *

13 I shall teach your ways to the wicked,
   and sinners shall return to you.

14 Deliver me from death, O God,
   and my tongue shall sing of your righteousness,
   O God of my salvation.

15 Open my lips, O Lord,
   and my mouth shall proclaim your praise.

16 Had you desired it, I would have offered sacrifice,
   but you take no delight in burnt-offerings.

17 The sacrifice of God is a troubled spirit;
   a broken and contrite heart, O God,
   you will not despise.

PSALM 53

1 The fool has said in his heart, 'There is no God'.
   All are corrupt and commit abominable acts;
   there is none who does any good.

2 God looks down from heaven upon us all,
   to see if there is any who is wise,
   if there is one who seeks after God.

3 Every one has proved faithless;
   all alike have turned bad;
   there is none who does good; no, not one.

4　Have they no knowledge, those evildoers
　　who eat up my people like bread
　　and do not call upon God?

5　See how greatly they tremble,
　　such trembling as never was;
　　for God has scattered the bones of the enemy;
　　they are put to shame,
　　because God has rejected them.

6　Oh, that Israel's deliverance would come out of Zion!
　　when God restores the fortunes of his people
　　Jacob will rejoice and Israel be glad.

PSALM 57

1　Be merciful to me, O God, be merciful,
　　for I have taken refuge in you;
　　in the shadow of your wings will I take refuge
　　until this time of trouble has gone by.

2　I will call upon the Most High God,
　　the God who maintains my cause.

3　He will send from heaven and save me;
　　he will confound those who trample upon me;
　　God will send forth his love and his faithfulness.

4　I lie in the midst of lions that devour the people;
　　their teeth are spears and arrows,
　　their tongue a sharp sword.

5　They have laid a net for my feet,
　　and I am bowed low;
　　they have dug a pit before me,
　　but have fallen into it themselves.

6   Exalt yourself above the heavens, O God,
      and your glory over all the earth.

7   My heart is firmly fixed, O God, my heart is fixed;
      I will sing and make melody.

8   Wake up, my spirit; awake, lute and harp;
      I myself will waken the dawn.

9   I will confess you among the peoples, O Lord;
      I will sing praise to you among the nations.

10   For your loving-kindness is greater than the heavens,
      and your faithfulness reaches to the clouds.

11   Exalt yourself above the heavens, O God,
      and your glory over all the earth.

PSALM 62:5-12

5   For God alone my soul in silence waits;
      truly, my hope is in him.

6   He alone is my rock and my salvation,
      my stronghold, so that I shall not be shaken.

7   In God is my safety and my honour;
      God is my strong rock and my refuge.

8   Put your trust in him always, O people,
      pour out your hearts before him,
      for God is our refuge.

9   Those of high degree are but a fleeting breath,
      even those of low estate cannot be trusted.

      On the scales they are lighter than a breath,
      all of them together.

10 Put no trust in extortion;
    in robbery take no empty pride;
        though wealth increase, set not your heart upon it.

11 God has spoken once, twice have I heard it,
        that power belongs to God.

12 Steadfast love is yours, O Lord,
        for you repay everyone according to their deeds.

PSALM 63:1-8

1 O God, you are my God; eagerly I seek you;
        my soul thirsts for you, my flesh faints for you,
        as in a barren and dry land where there is no water.

2 Therefore I have gazed upon you in your holy place,
        that I might behold your power and your glory.

3 For your loving-kindness is better than life itself;
        my lips shall give you praise.

4 So will I bless you as long as I live
        and lift up my hands in your name.

5 My soul is content, as with marrow and fatness,
        and my mouth praises you with joyful lips,

6 When I remember you upon my bed,
        and meditate on you in the night watches.

7 For you have been my helper,
        and under the shadow of your wings I will rejoice.

8 My soul clings to you;
        your right hand holds me fast.

PSALM 65

1 You are to be praised, O God, in Zion;
   to you shall vows be performed in Jerusalem.

2 To you that hear prayer shall all flesh come,
   because of their transgressions.

3 Our sins are stronger than we are,
   but you will blot them out.

4 Happy are they whom you choose
   and draw to your courts to dwell there!
   they will be satisfied by the beauty of your house,
   by the holiness of your temple.

5 Awesome things will you show us in your righteousness,
   O God of our salvation,
   O Hope of all the ends of the earth
   and of the seas that are far away.

6 You make fast the mountains by your power;
   they are girded about with might.

7 You still the roaring of the seas,
   the roaring of their waves,
   and the clamour of the peoples.

8 Those who dwell at the ends of the earth
   will tremble at your marvellous signs;
   you make the dawn and the dusk to sing for joy.

*   *   *

9 You visit the earth and water it abundantly;
   you make it very plenteous;
   the river of God is full of water.

   You prepare the grain,
   for so you provide for the earth.

10   You drench the furrows and smooth out the ridges;
       with heavy rain you soften the ground
       and bless its increase.

11   You crown the year with your goodness,
       and your paths overflow with plenty.

12   May the fields of the wilderness be rich for grazing,
       and the hills be clothed with joy.

13   May the meadows cover themselves with flocks,
       and the valleys cloak themselves with grain;
       let them shout for joy and sing.

PSALM 66:8-20

 8   Bless our God, you peoples;
       make the voice of his praise to be heard;

 9   Who holds our souls in life,
       and will not allow our feet to slip.

10   For you, O God, have proved us;
       you have tried us just as silver is tried.

11   You brought us into the snare;
       you laid heavy burdens upon our backs.

12   You let enemies ride over our heads;
       we went through fire and water;
       but you brought us out into a place of refreshment.

13   I will enter your house with burnt-offerings
       and will pay you my vows,
14   **which I promised with my lips**
       and spoke with my mouth when I was in trouble.

15 I will offer you sacrifices of fat beasts
    with the smoke of rams;
        I will give you oxen and goats.

16 Come and listen, all you who fear God,
        and I will tell you what he has done for me.

17 I called out to him with my mouth,
        and his praise was on my tongue.

18 If I had found evil in my heart,
        the Lord would not have heard me;

19 But in truth God has heard me;
        he has attended to the voice of my prayer.

20 Blessed be God, who has not rejected my prayer,
        nor withheld his love from me.

PSALM 67

1 May God be merciful to us and bless us,
        show us the light of his countenance and come to us.

2 Let your ways be known upon earth,
        your saving health among all nations.

3 Let the peoples praise you, O God;
        let all the peoples praise you.

4 Let the nations be glad and sing for joy,
        **for you judge the peoples with equity
        and guide all the nations upon earth.**

5 Let the peoples praise you, O God;
        let all the peoples praise you.

6   The earth has brought forth her increase;
    may God, our own God, give us his blessing.

7   May God give us his blessing,
    **and may all the ends of the earth
    stand in awe of him.**

PSALM 68:1-10

1   Let God arise, and let his enemies be scattered;
    let those who hate him flee before him.

2   Let them vanish like smoke when the wind drives it away;
    **as the wax melts at the fire,
    so let the wicked perish at the presence of God.**

3   But let the righteous be glad and rejoice before God;
    let them also be merry and joyful.

4   Sing to God, sing praises to his name;
    exalt him who rides upon the heavens;
    Yahweh is his name, rejoice before him!

5   Father of orphans, defender of widows,
    God in his holy habitation!

6   God gives the solitary a home
    and brings forth prisoners into freedom;
    but the rebels shall live in dry places.

7   O God, when you went forth before your people,
    when you marched through the wilderness,

8   The earth shook, and the skies poured down rain,
    at the presence of God, the God of Sinai,
    at the presence of God, the God of Israel.

9   You sent a gracious rain, O God, upon your inheritance;
      you refreshed the land when it was weary.

10   Your people found their home in it;
      in your goodness, O God,
      you have made provision for the poor.

PSALM 69:6-15

6   Let not those who hope in you
      be put to shame through me, Lord God of hosts;
      let not those who seek you be disgraced because of me,
      O God of Israel.

7   Surely, for your sake have I suffered reproach,
      and shame has covered my face.

8   I have become a stranger to my own kindred,
      an alien to my mother's children.

9   Zeal for your house has eaten me up;
      the scorn of those who scorn you has fallen upon me.

10   I humbled myself with fasting,
      but that was turned to my reproach.

11   I put on sack-cloth also,
      and became a byword among them.

12   Those who sit at the gate murmur against me,
      and the drunkards make songs about me.

13   But as for me, this is my prayer to you,
      at the time you have set, O Lord:

14   'In your great mercy, O God,
      answer me with your unfailing help.

Save me from the mire; do not let me sink;
   **let me be rescued from those who hate me
   and out of the deep waters.**

15 Let not the torrent of waters wash over me,
   neither let the deep swallow me up;
      do not let the Pit shut its mouth upon me'.

PSALM 70

1 Be pleased, O God, to deliver me;
      O Lord, make haste to help me.

2 Let those who seek my life be ashamed
   and altogether dismayed;
      **let those who take pleasure in my misfortune
      draw back and be disgraced.**

3 Let those who say to me 'Aha!'
   and gloat over me turn back,
      because they are ashamed.

4 Let all who seek you rejoice and be glad in you;
      **let those who love your salvation say for ever,
      'Great is the Lord!'**

5 But as for me, I am poor and needy;
      come to me speedily, O God.

   You are my helper and my deliverer;
      O Lord, do not delay.

PSALM 71:1-12

1   In you, O Lord, have I taken refuge;
       let me never be ashamed;

2   In your righteousness, deliver me and set me free;
       incline your ear to me and save me.

3   Be my strong rock, a castle to keep me safe;
       you are my crag and my stronghold.

4   Deliver me, my God, from the hand of the wicked,
       from the clutches of the evildoer and the oppressor.

5   For you are my hope, O Lord God,
       my confidence since I was young.

6   I have been sustained by you ever since I was born;
       from my mother's womb you have been my strength;
       my praise shall be always of you.

                *   *   *

7   I have become a portent to many;
       but you are my refuge and strength.

8   Let my mouth be full of your praise
       and your glory all the day long.

9   Do not cast me off in my old age;
       forsake me not when my strength fails.

10   For my enemies are talking against me,
       and those who lie in wait for my life
       take counsel together.

11   They say, 'God has forsaken him;
       go after him and seize him;
       because there is none who will save'.

12   O God, be not far from me;
       come quickly to help me, O my God.

PSALM 72:1-14

1   Give the king your justice, O God,
    and your righteousness to the king's son;

2   That he may rule your people righteously
    and the poor with justice;

3   That the mountains may bring prosperity to the people,
    and the little hills bring righteousness.

4   He shall defend the needy among the people;
    he shall rescue the poor and crush the oppressor.

5   He shall live as long as the sun and the moon endure,
    from one generation to another.

6   He shall come down like rain upon the mown field,
    like showers that water the earth.

7   In his time shall the righteous flourish;
    there shall be abundance of peace
    till the moon shall be no more.

8   He shall rule from sea to sea,
    and from the River to the ends of the earth.

        *   *   *

9   His foes shall bow down before him,
    and his enemies lick the dust.

10 The kings of Tarshish and of the isles shall pay tribute,
    and the kings of Arabia and Saba offer gifts.

11 All kings shall bow down before him,
    and all the nations do him service.

12 For he shall deliver the poor who cries out in distress,
    and the oppressed who has no helper.

13 He shall have pity on the lowly and poor;
    he shall preserve the lives of the needy.

14 He shall redeem their lives from oppression and violence,
    and dear shall their blood be in his sight.

PSALM 76

1 In Judah is God known;
   his name is great in Israel.

2 At Salem is his tabernacle,
   and his dwelling is in Zion.

3 There he broke the flashing arrows,
   the shield, the sword, and the weapons of battle.

4 How glorious you are!
   more splendid than the everlasting mountains!

5 The strong of heart have been despoiled;
   they sink into sleep;
   none of the warriors can lift a hand.

6 At your rebuke, O God of Jacob,
   both horse and rider lie stunned.

7 What terror you inspire!
   who can stand before you when you are angry?

8 From heaven you pronounced judgment;
   the earth was afraid and was still;

9 When God rose up to judgment
   and to save all the oppressed of the earth.

10   Truly, wrathful Edom will give you thanks,
and the remnant of Hamath will keep your feasts.

11   Make a vow to the Lord your God and keep it;
let all around him bring gifts to him
who is worthy to be feared.

12   He breaks the spirit of princes,
and strikes terror in the kings of the earth.

PSALM 77:11-20

11   I will remember the works of the Lord,
and call to mind your wonders of old time.

12   I will meditate on all your acts
and ponder your mighty deeds.

13   Your way, O God, is holy;
who is so great a god as our God?

14   You are the God who works wonders
and have declared your power among the peoples.

15   By your strength you have redeemed your people,
the children of Jacob and Joseph.

16   The waters saw you, O God;
the waters saw you and trembled;
the very depths were shaken.

17   The clouds poured out water;
the skies thundered;
your arrows flashed to and fro;

18   The sound of your thunder was in the whirlwind;
your lightnings lit up the world;
the earth trembled and shook.

19 Your way was in the sea,
   and your paths in the great waters,
   yet your footsteps were not seen.

20 You led your people like a flock
   by the hand of Moses and Aaron.

PSALM 78:1-3, 10-20

1 Hear my teaching, O my people;
  incline your ears to the words of my mouth.

2 I will open my mouth in a parable;
  I will declare the mysteries of ancient times.

3 That which we have heard and known,
  and what our forebears have told us.

10 They did not keep the covenant of God,
   and refused to walk in his law;

11 They forgot what he had done,
   and the wonders he had shown them.

12 He worked marvels in the sight of their forebears,
   in the land of Egypt, in the field of Zoan.

13 He split open the sea and let them pass through;
   he made the waters stand up like walls.

14 He led them with a cloud by day,
   and all the night through with a glow of fire.

15 He split the hard rocks in the wilderness
   and gave them drink as from the great deep.

16 He brought streams out of the cliff,
   and the waters gushed out like rivers.

17 But they went on sinning against him,
   rebelling in the desert against the Most High.

18 They tested God in their hearts,
   demanding food for their craving.

19 They railed against God and said,
   'Can God set a table in the wilderness?

20 True, he struck the rock, the waters gushed out,
   and the gullies overflowed;
   but is he able to give bread
   or to provide meat for his people?'

PSALM 80:1-7

1 Hear, O Shepherd of Israel, leading Joseph like a flock;
   shine forth,
   you that are enthroned upon the cherubim.

2 In the presence of Ephraim, Benjamin, and Manasseh,
   stir up your strength and come to help us.

3 Restore us, O God of hosts;
   show the light of your countenance,
   and we shall be saved.

4 O Lord God of hosts,
   how long will you be angered
   despite the prayers of your people?

5 You have fed them with the bread of tears;
   you have given them bowls of tears to drink.

6 You have made us the derision of our neighbours,
   and our enemies laugh us to scorn.

7 Restore us, O God of hosts;
   show the light of your countenance,
   and we shall be saved.

PSALM 81:1-10

1 Sing with joy to God our strength
 and raise a loud shout to the God of Jacob.

2 Raise a song and sound the timbrel,
 the merry harp, and the lyre.

3 Blow the ram's-horn at the new moon,
 and at the full moon, the day of our feast.

4 For this is a statute for Israel,
 a law of the God of Jacob.

5 He laid it as a solemn charge upon Joseph,
 when he came out of the land of Egypt.

6 I heard an unfamiliar voice saying,
 'I eased his shoulder from the burden;
 his hands were set free from bearing the load'.

7 You called on me in trouble, and I saved you;
 I answered you from the secret place of thunder
 and tested you at the waters of Meribah.

8 Hear, O my people, and I will admonish you;
 O Israel, if you would but listen to me!

9 There shall be no strange god among you;
 you shall not worship a foreign god.

10 I am the Lord your God,
 who brought you out of the land of Egypt and said,
 'Open your mouth wide, and I will fill it'.

PSALM 82

1 God takes his stand in the council of heaven;
 he gives judgment in the midst of the gods:

2   'How long will you judge unjustly,
    and show favour to the wicked?

3   Save the weak and the orphan;
    defend the humble and needy.

4   Rescue the weak and the poor;
    deliver them from the power of the wicked.

5   They do not know, neither do they understand;
    they go about in darkness;
    all the foundations of the earth are shaken.

6   Now I say to you, "You are gods,
    and all of you children of the Most High;

7   Nevertheless, you shall die like mortals,
    and fall like any prince".

8   Arise, O God, and rule the earth,
    for you shall take all nations for your own.

PSALM 84

1   How dear to me is your dwelling, O Lord of hosts!
2   **My soul has a desire and longing**
    for the courts of the Lord;
    my heart and my flesh rejoice in the living God.

3   The sparrow has found her a house
    and the swallow a nest where she may lay her young;
    by the side of your altars, O Lord of hosts,
    my King and my God.

4   Happy are they who dwell in your house!
    they will always be praising you.

5   Happy are the people whose strength is in you!
    whose hearts are set on the pilgrims' way.

6 Those who go through the desolate valley
   will find it a place of springs,
     for the early rains have covered it with pools of water.

7 They will climb from height to height,
     and the God of gods will reveal himself in Zion.

8 Lord God of hosts, hear my prayer;
     give ear, O God of Jacob.

9 Behold our defender, O God;
     and look upon the face of your anointed.

10 For one day in your courts
    is better than a thousand in my own room,
      and to stand at the threshold of the house of my God
      than to dwell in the tents of the wicked.

11 For the Lord God is both sun and shield;
      he will give grace and glory;

    No good thing will the Lord withhold
      from those who walk with integrity.

12 O Lord of hosts,
      happy are they who put their trust in you!

PSALM 85:8-13

8 I will listen to what the Lord God is saying,
     for he is speaking peace to his faithful people
     and to those who turn their hearts to him.

9 Truly, his salvation is very near to those who fear him,
     that his glory may dwell in our land.

10 Mercy and truth have met together;
      righteousness and peace have kissed each other.

11 Truth shall spring up from the earth,
      and righteousness shall look down from heaven.

12 The Lord will indeed grant prosperity,
   and our land will yield its increase.

13 Righteousness shall go before him,
   and peace shall be a pathway for his feet.

PSALM 89: 1-4, 19-37

1 Your love, O Lord, for ever will I sing;
   **from age to age
   my mouth will proclaim your faithfulness.**

2 For I am persuaded that your love is established for ever;
   you have set your faithfulness firmly in the heavens.

3 'I have made a covenant with my chosen one;
   I have sworn an oath to David my servant.

4 I will establish your line for ever,
   and preserve your throne for all generations.'

19 You spoke once in a vision
   and said to your faithful people:
   **'I have set the crown upon a warrior
   and have exalted one chosen out of the people.**

        *   *   *

20 I have found David my servant;
   with my holy oil have I anointed him.

21 My hand will hold him fast
   and my arm will make him strong.

22 No enemy shall deceive him,
   nor any wicked man bring him down.

23   I will crush his foes before him
       and strike down those who hate him.

24   My faithfulness and love shall be with him,
       and he shall be victorious through my name.

            *   *   *

25   I shall make his dominion extend
       from the Great Sea to the River.

26   He will say to me, "You are my Father,
       my God, and the rock of my salvation".

27   I will make him my firstborn
       and higher than the kings of the earth.

28   I will keep my love for him for ever,
       and my covenant will stand firm for him.

29   I will establish his line for ever
       and his throne as the days of heaven.

30   If his children forsake my law
       and do not walk according to my judgments;

31   If they break my statutes
       and do not keep my commandments;

32   I will punish their transgressions with a rod
       and their iniquities with the lash;

33   But I will not take my love from him,
       nor let my faithfulness prove false.

34   I will not break my covenant,
       nor change what has gone out of my lips.

35   Once for all I have sworn by my holiness:
       I will not lie to David.

36   His line shall endure for ever
     and his throne as the sun before me;

37   It shall stand fast for evermore like the moon,
     the abiding witness in the sky'.

PSALM 90

1   Lord, you have been our refuge
     from one generation to another.

2   Before the mountains were brought forth,
     or the land and the earth were born,
     from age to age you are God.

3   You turn us back to the dust and say,
     'Go back, O child of earth'.

4   For a thousand years in your sight
     are like yesterday when it is past
     and like a watch in the night.

5   You sweep us away like a dream;
     we fade away suddenly like the grass.

6   In the morning it is green and flourishes;
     in the evening it is dried up and withered.

7   For we consume away in your displeasure;
     we are afraid because of your wrathful indignation.

8   Our iniquities you have set before you,
     and our secret sins in the light of your countenance.

9   When you are angry, all our days are gone;
     we bring our years to an end like a sigh.

10 The span of our life is seventy years,
     perhaps in strength even eighty;
     yet the sum of them is but labour and sorrow,
     for they pass away quickly and we are gone.

11   Who regards the power of your wrath?
      who rightly fears your indignation?

12   So teach us to number our days
      that we may apply our hearts to wisdom.

          *   *   *

13   Return, O Lord; how long will you delay?
      be gracious to your servants.

14   Satisfy us by your loving-kindness in the morning;
      so shall we rejoice and be glad all the days of our life.

15   Make us glad by the measure of the days
      that you afflicted us
      and the years in which we suffered adversity.

16   Show your servants your works
      and your splendour to their children.

17   May the graciousness of the Lord our God be upon us;
      prosper the work of our hands;
      prosper our handiwork.

PSALM 91

1   Those who dwell in the shelter of the Most High,
      abide under the shadow of the Almighty.

2   They shall say to the Lord,
      'You are my refuge and my stronghold,
      my God in whom I put my trust'.

3   He shall deliver you from the snare of the hunter
      and from the deadly pestilence.

4   He shall cover you with his pinions,
      and you shall find refuge under his wings;
      his faithfulness shall be a shield and buckler.

5   You shall not be afraid of any terror by night,
       nor of the arrow that flies by day;

6   Of the plague that stalks in the darkness,
       nor of the sickness that lays waste at mid-day.

7   A thousand shall fall at your side
     and ten thousand at your right hand,
       but it shall not come near you.

8   Your eyes have only to behold
       to see the reward of the wicked.
              *   *   *
9   Because you have made the Lord your refuge,
       and the Most High your habitation,

10   There shall no evil happen to you,
       neither shall any plague come near your dwelling.
              *   *   *
11   For he shall give his angels charge over you,
       to keep you in all your ways.

12   They shall bear you in their hands,
       lest you dash your foot against a stone.

13   You shall tread upon the lion and adder;
       **you shall trample the young lion and the serpent
       under your feet.**

14   Because they are bound to me in love,
     therefore will I deliver them;
       I will protect them, because they know my name.

15   They shall call upon me, and I will answer them;
       **I am with them in trouble;
       I will rescue them and bring them to honour.**

16   With long life will I satisfy them,
       and show them my salvation.

PSALM 92: 1-4, 12-15

1   It is a good thing to give thanks to the Lord,
    and to sing praises to your name, O Most High;

2   To tell of your loving-kindness early in the morning
    and of your faithfulness in the night season;

3   On the psaltery, and on the lyre,
    and to the melody of the harp.

4   For you have made me glad by your acts, O Lord;
    and I shout for joy
    because of the works of your hands.

12   The righteous shall flourish like a palm tree,
    and shall spread abroad like a cedar of Lebanon.

13   Those who are planted in the house of the Lord
    shall flourish in the courts of our God;

14   They shall still bear fruit in old age;
    they shall be green and succulent;

15   That they may show how upright the Lord is,
    my rock, in whom there is no fault.

PSALM 93

1   The Lord is king;
    he has put on splendid apparel;
    the Lord has put on his apparel
    and girded himself with strength.
    He has made the whole world so sure
    that it cannot be moved;

2   Ever since the world began,
    your throne has been established;
    you are from everlasting.

3   The waters have lifted up, O Lord,
    the waters have lifted up their voice;
    the waters have lifted up their pounding waves.

4　Mightier than the sound of many waters,
　　mightier than the breakers of the sea,
　　　mightier is the Lord who dwells on high.

5　Your testimonies are very sure,
　　　and holiness adorns your house, O Lord,
　　　for ever and for evermore.

PSALM 94:12-22

12　Happy are they whom you instruct, O Lord!
　　　whom you teach out of your law;

13　To give them rest in evil days,
　　　until a pit is dug for the wicked.

14　For the Lord will not abandon his people,
　　　nor will he forsake his own.

15　For judgment will again be just,
　　　and all the true of heart will follow it.

16　Who rose up for me against the wicked?
　　　who took my part against the evildoers?

17　If the Lord had not come to my help,
　　　I should soon have dwelt in the land of silence.

18　As often as I said, 'My foot has slipped',
　　　your love, O Lord, upheld me.

19　When many cares fill my mind,
　　　your consolations cheer my soul.

20　Can a corrupt tribunal have any part with you,
　　　one which frames evil into law?

21 They conspire against the life of the just
      and condemn the innocent to death.

22 But the Lord has become my stronghold,
      and my God the rock of my trust.

PSALM 95

1 Come, let us sing to the Lord;
     let us shout for joy to the rock of our salvation.

2 Let us come before his presence with thanksgiving
     and raise a loud shout to him with psalms.

3 For the Lord is a great God,
     and a great king above all gods.

4 In his hand are the caverns of the earth,
     and the heights of the hills are his also.

5 The sea is his, for he made it,
     and his hands have moulded the dry land.

6 Come, let us bow down, and bend the knee,
     and kneel before the Lord our Maker.

7 For he is our God,
     and we are the people of his pasture
     and the sheep of his hand,
     Oh, that today you would hearken to his voice!

8 Harden not your hearts,
     as your forebears did in the wilderness,
     at Meribah, and on that day at Massah,
     when they tempted me.

9 They put me to the test,
     though they had seen my works.

10　Forty years long I detested that generation and said,
　　　'This people are wayward in their hearts;
　　　they do not know my ways'.

11　So I swore in my wrath,
　　　'They shall not enter into my rest'.

PSALM 96

1　Sing to the Lord a new song;
　　　sing to the Lord, all the whole earth.

2　Sing to the Lord and bless his name;
　　　proclaim the good news of his salvation
　　　from day to day.

3　Declare his glory among the nations
　　　and his wonders among all peoples.

4　For great is the Lord and greatly to be praised;
　　　he is more to be feared than all gods.

5　As for all the gods of the nations, they are but idols;
　　　but it is the Lord who made the heavens.

6　Oh, the majesty and magnificence of his presence!
　　　Oh, the power and the splendour of his sanctuary!

7　Ascribe to the Lord, you families of the peoples;
　　　ascribe to the Lord honour and power.

8　Ascribe to the Lord the honour due to his name;
　　　bring offerings and come into his courts.

9　Worship the Lord in the beauty of holiness;
　　　let the whole earth tremble before him.

10　Tell it out among the nations: 'The Lord is king!
　　　he has made the world so firm
　　　that it cannot be moved;
　　　he will judge the peoples with equity'.

11   Let the heavens rejoice, and let the earth be glad;
let the sea thunder and all that is in it;

12   **let the field be joyful and all that is therein.**

Then shall all the trees of the wood shout for joy

13   before the Lord when he comes,
     ˙when he comes to judge the earth.

He will judge the world with righteousness
and the peoples with his truth.

PSALM 97

1   The Lord is king;
let the earth rejoice;
    let the multitude of the isles be glad.

2   Clouds and darkness are round about him,
    righteousness and justice
    are the foundations of his throne.

3   A fire goes before him
    and burns up his enemies on every side.

4   His lightnings light up the world;
    the earth sees it and is afraid.

5   The mountains melt like wax at the presence of the Lord,
    at the presence of the Lord of the whole earth.

6   The heavens declare his righteousness,
    and all the peoples see his glory.

7   Confounded be all who worship carved images
and delight in false gods!
    Bow down before him, all you gods.

8   Zion hears and is glad, and the cities of Judah rejoice,
      because of your judgments, O Lord.

9   For you are the Lord,
    most high over all the earth;
      you are exalted far above all gods.

10   The Lord loves those who hate evil;
      he preserves the lives of his saints
      and delivers them from the hand of the wicked.

11   Light has sprung up for the righteous,
      and joyful gladness for those who are truehearted.

12   Rejoice in the Lord, you righteous,
      and give thanks to his holy name.

PSALM 98

1   Sing to the Lord a new song,
      for he has done marvellous things.

2   With his right hand and his holy arm
      has he won for himself the victory.

    The Lord has made known his victory;
      his righteousness has he openly shown
      in the sight of the nations.

3   He remembers his mercy and faithfulness
    to the house of Israel,
      and all the ends of the earth
      have seen the victory of our God.

4 Shout with joy to the Lord, all you lands;
   lift up your voice, rejoice, and sing.

5 Sing to the Lord with the harp,
   with the harp and the voice of song.

6 With trumpets and the sound of the horn
   shout with joy before the King, the Lord.

7 Let the sea make a noise and all that is in it,
   the lands and those who dwell therein.

8 Let the rivers clap their hands,
   and let the hills ring out with joy before the Lord,
   when he comes to judge the earth.

9 In righteousness shall he judge the world
   and the peoples with equity.

PSALM 99

1 The Lord is king;
   let the earth tremble;
   he is enthroned upon the cherubim;
   let the earth shake.

2 The Lord is great in Zion;
   he is high above all peoples.

3 Let them confess his name, which is great and awesome;
   he is the Holy One.

4 'O mighty King, lover of justice,
   you have established equity;
   you have executed justice and righteousness in Jacob.'

5 Proclaim the greatness of the Lord our God
   and fall down before his footstool;
   he is the Holy One.

6   Moses and Aaron among his priests,
    and Samuel among those who call upon his name,
      they called upon the Lord, and he answered them.

7   He spoke to them out of the pillar of cloud;
      they kept his testimonies
      and the decree that he gave them.

8   'O Lord our God, you answered them indeed;
      you were a God who forgave them,
      yet punished them for their evil deeds.'

9   Proclaim the greatness of the Lord our God
    and worship him upon his holy hill;
      for the Lord our God is the Holy One.

PSALM 100

1   Be joyful in the Lord, all you lands;
2   **serve the Lord with gladness**
      and come before his presence with a song.

3   Know this: The Lord himself is God;
      he has made us, and we are his;
      we are his people and the sheep of his pasture.

4   Enter his gates with thanksgiving;
    go into his courts with praise;
      give thanks to him and call upon his name.

5   For the Lord is good;
    his mercy is everlasting;
      and his faithfulness endures from age to age.

PSALM 101

1 I will sing of mercy and justice;
   to you, O Lord, will I sing praises.

2 I will strive to follow a blameless course;
   oh, when will you come to me?
   I will walk with sincerity of heart within my house.

3 I will set no worthless thing before my eyes;
   I hate the doers of evil deeds;
   they shall not remain with me.

4 A crooked heart shall be far from me;
   I will not know evil.

5 Those who in secret slander their neighbours
   I will destroy;
   those who have a haughty look and a proud heart
   I cannot abide.

6 My eyes are upon the faithful in the land,
   that they may dwell with me,
   and only those who lead a blameless life
   shall be my servants.

7 Those who act deceitfully shall not dwell in my house,
   and those who tell lies shall not continue in my sight.

8 I will soon destroy all the wicked in the land,
   that I may root out all evildoers
   from the city of the Lord.

PSALM 102:1-12

1 Lord, hear my prayer, and let my cry come before you;
2 **hide not your face from me in the day of my trouble.**

   Incline your ear to me;
   when I call, make haste to answer me.

3   For my days drift away like smoke,
     and my bones are hot as burning coals.

4   My heart is smitten like grass and withered,
     so that I forget to eat my bread.

5   Because of the voice of my groaning
     I am but skin and bones.

6   I have become like a vulture in the wilderness,
     like an owl among the ruins.

7   I lie awake and groan;
     I am like a sparrow, lonely on a house-top.

8   My enemies revile me all day long,
     and those who scoff at me
     have taken an oath against me.

9   For I have eaten ashes for bread
     and mingled my drink with weeping.

10 Because of your indignation and wrath
     you have lifted me up and thrown me away.

11 My days pass away like a shadow,
     and I wither like the grass.

12 But you, O Lord, endure for ever,
     and your name from age to age.

PSALM 103:1-13

1   Bless the Lord, O my soul,
     and all that is within me, bless his holy name.

2   Bless the Lord, O my soul,
     and forget not all his benefits.

3   He forgives all your sins
     and heals all your infirmities;

4   He redeems your life from the grave
         and crowns you with mercy and loving-kindness;

5   He satisfies you with good things,
         and your youth is renewed like an eagle's.

6   The Lord executes righteousness
         and judgment for all who are oppressed.

7   He made his ways known to Moses
         and his works to the children of Israel.

8   The Lord is full of compassion and mercy,
         slow to anger and of great kindness.

9   He will not always accuse us,
         nor will he keep his anger for ever.

10   He has not dealt with us according to our sins,
         nor rewarded us according to our wickedness.

11   For as the heavens are high above the earth,
         so is his mercy great upon those who fear him.

12   As far as the east is from the west,
         so far has he removed our sins from us.

13   As a father cares for his children,
         so does the Lord care for those who fear him.

PSALM 104:24-34

24   O Lord, how manifold are your works!
         in wisdom you have made them all;
         the earth is full of your creatures.

25   Yonder is the great and wide sea
         with its living things too many to number,
         creatures both small and great.

26 There move the ships,
    and there is that Leviathan,
      which you have made for the sport of it.

27 All of them look to you
      to give them their food in due season.

28 You give it to them; they gather it;
      you open your hand,
      and they are filled with good things.

29 You hide your face, and they are terrified;
      you take away their breath,
      and they die and return to their dust.

30 You send forth your Spirit, and they are created;
      and so you renew the face of the earth.

31 May the glory of the Lord endure for ever;
      may the Lord rejoice in all his works.

32 He looks at the earth and it trembles;
      he touches the mountains and they smoke.

33 I will sing to the Lord as long as I live;
      I will praise my God while I have my being.

34 May these words of mine please him;
      I will rejoice in the Lord.

PSALM 105:1-11

1   Give thanks to the Lord and call upon his name;
      make known his deeds among the peoples.

2   Sing to him, sing praises to him,
      and speak of all his marvellous works.

3   Glory in his holy name;
      let the hearts of those who seek the Lord rejoice.

4   Search for the Lord and his strength;
    continually seek his face.

5   Remember the marvels he has done,
    his wonders and the judgments of his mouth,

6   O offspring of Abraham his servant,
    O children of Jacob his chosen.

7   He is the Lord our God;
    his judgments prevail in all the world.

8   He has always been mindful of his covenant,
    the promise he made for a thousand generations.

9   The covenant he made with Abraham,
    the oath that he swore to Isaac,

10 Which he established as a statute for Jacob,
    an everlasting covenant for Israel,

11 Saying, 'To you will I give the land of Canaan
    to be your allotted inheritance'.

PSALM 106: 4-12, 19-23

4   Remember me, O Lord,
    with the favour you have for your people,
    and visit me with your saving help.

5   That I may see the prosperity of your elect
    and be glad with the gladness of your people,
    that I may glory with your inheritance.

6   We have sinned as our forebears did;
    we have done wrong and dealt wickedly.

*   *   *

7   In Egypt they did not consider your marvellous works,
    nor remember the abundance of your love;
      they defied the Most High at the Red Sea.

8   But he saved them for his name's sake,
      to make his power known.

                    *   *   *

9   He rebuked the Red Sea, and it dried up,
      and he led them through the deep
      as through a desert.

10 He saved them from the hand of those who hated them
      and redeemed them from the hand of the enemy.

11 The waters covered their oppressors;
      not one of them was left.

12 Then they believed his words
      and sang him songs of praise.

                    *   *   *

19 Israel made a bull-calf at Horeb
      and worshipped a molten image;

20 And so they exchanged their glory
      for the image of an ox that feeds on grass.

21 They forgot God their saviour,
      who had done great things in Egypt,

22 Wonderful deeds in the land of Ham,
      and fearful things at the Red Sea.

23 So he would have destroyed them,
    had not Moses his chosen stood before him in the breach,
      to turn away his wrath from consuming them.

PSALM 107:1-9, 33-43

1   Give thanks to the Lord, for he is good,
    and his mercy endures for ever.

2   Let all those whom the Lord has redeemed proclaim
    that he redeemed them from the hand of the foe.

3   He gathered them out of the lands;
    from the east and from the west,
    from the north and from the south.

4   Some wandered in desert wastes;
    they found no way to a city where they might dwell.

5   They were hungry and thirsty;
    their spirits languished within them.

6   Then they cried to the Lord in their trouble,
    and he delivered them from their distress.

7   He put their feet on a straight path
    to go to a city where they might dwell.

8   Let them give thanks to the Lord for his mercy
    and the wonders he does for his children.

9   For he satisfies the thirsty
    and fills the hungry with good things.

33   The Lord changed rivers into deserts,
    and water-springs into thirsty ground,

34   A fruitful land into salt flats,
    because of the wickedness of those who dwell there.

35   He changed deserts into pools of water
    and dry land into water-springs.

36 He settled the hungry there,
   and they founded a city to dwell in.

37 They sowed fields, and planted vineyards,
   and brought in a fruitful harvest.

38 He blessed them, so that they increased greatly,
   he did not let their herds decrease.

39 Yet when they were diminished and brought low,
   through stress of adversity and sorrow,

40 (He pours contempt on princes
   and makes them wander in trackless wastes)

41 He lifted up the poor out of misery
   and multiplied their families like flocks of sheep.

42 The upright will see this and rejoice,
   but all wickedness will shut its mouth.

43 Whoever is wise will ponder these things,
   and consider well the mercies of the Lord.

PSALM 111

1 Hallelujah!
  I will give thanks to the Lord with my whole heart,
   in the assembly of the upright, in the congregation.

2 Great are the deeds of the Lord!
   they are studied by all who delight in them.

3 His work is full of majesty and splendour
   and his righteousness endures for ever.

4 He makes his marvellous works to be remembered;
   the Lord is gracious and full of compassion.

5 He gives good to those who fear him;
   he is ever mindful of his covenant.

6   He has shown his people the power of his works
       in giving them the lands of the nations.

7   The works of his hands are faithfulness and justice;
       all his commandments are sure.

8   They stand fast for ever and ever,
       because they are done in truth and equity.

9   He sent redemption to his people;
    he commanded his covenant for ever;
       holy and awesome is his name.

10   The fear of the Lord is the beginning of wisdom;
       those who act accordingly have a good understanding;
       his praise endures for ever.

PSALM 112:4-9

4   Light shines in the darkness for the upright;
       the righteous are merciful and full of compassion.

5   It is good for them to be generous in lending
       and to manage their affairs with justice.

6   For they will never be shaken;
       the righteous will be kept in everlasting remembrance.

7   They will not be afraid of any evil rumours;
       their heart is right;
       they put their trust in the Lord.

8   Their heart is established and will not shrink,
       until they see their desire upon their enemies.

9   They have given freely to the poor,
       and their righteousness stands fast for ever;
       they will hold up their head with honour.

PSALM 113

1 Hallelujah!
Give praise, you servants of the Lord;
  praise the name of the Lord.

2 Let the name of the Lord be blessed,
  from this time forth for evermore.

3 From the rising of the sun to its going down
  let the name of the Lord be praised.

4 The Lord is high above all nations,
  and his glory above the heavens.

5 Who is like the Lord our God, who sits enthroned on high,
6 **but stoops to behold the heavens and the earth?**

7 He takes up the weak out of the dust
  and lifts up the poor from the ashes.

8 He sets them with the princes,
  with the princes of his people.

9 He makes the woman of a childless house
  to be a joyful mother of children.

PSALM 114

1 Hallelujah!
When Israel came out of Egypt,
  the house of Jacob from a people of strange speech,

2 Judah became God's sanctuary
  and Israel his dominion.

3 The sea beheld it and fled;
  Jordan turned and went back.

4   The mountains skipped like rams,
     and the little hills like young sheep.

5   What ailed you, O sea, that you fled?
     O Jordan, that you turned back?

6   You mountains, that you skipped like rams?
     you little hills like young sheep?

7   Tremble, O earth, at the presence of the Lord,
     at the presence of the God of Jacob.

8   Who turned the hard rock into a pool of water
     and flint-stone into a flowing spring.

PSALM 115: 1-11

1   Not to us, O Lord, not to us,
     but to your name give glory;
     because of your love and because of your faithfulness.

2   Why should the heathen say,
     `'Where then is their God?'**

3   Our God is in heaven;
     whatever he wills to do he does.

4   Their idols are silver and gold,
     the work of human hands.

5   They have mouths, but they cannot speak;
     eyes have they, but they cannot see;

6   They have ears, but they cannot hear;
     noses, but they cannot smell;

7   They have hands, but they cannot feel;
     feet, but they cannot walk;
     they make no sound with their throat.

8   Those who make them are like them,
     and so are all who put their trust in them.

9   O Israel, trust in the Lord;
     he is their help and their shield.

10   O house of Aaron, trust in the Lord;
     he is their help and their shield.

11   You who fear the Lord, trust in the Lord;
     he is their help and their shield.

PSALM 116: 1-9, 12-19

1   I love the Lord,
     because he has heard the voice of my supplication,
2   **because he has inclined his ear to me**
     whenever I called upon him.

3   The cords of death entangled me;
     the grip of the grave took hold of me;
     I came to grief and sorrow.

4   Then I called upon the name of the Lord:
     'O Lord, I pray you, save my life'.

5   Gracious is the Lord and righteous;
     our God is full of compassion.

6   The Lord watches over the innocent;
     I was brought very low, and he helped me.

7   Turn again to your rest, O my soul,
     for the Lord has treated you well.

8   For you have rescued my life from death,
     my eyes from tears, and my feet from stumbling.

9   I will walk in the presence of the Lord
    in the land of the living.

              *   *   *

12 How shall I repay the Lord
    for all the good things he has done for me?

13 I will lift up the cup of salvation
    and call upon the name of the Lord.

14 I will fulfil my vows to the Lord
    in the presence of all his people.

15 Precious in the sight of the Lord
    is the death of his servants.

16 O Lord, I am your servant;
    **I am your servant and the child of your handmaid;
    you have freed me from my bonds.**

17 I will offer you the sacrifice of thanksgiving
    and call upon the name of the Lord.

18 I will fulfil my vows to the Lord
    in the presence of all his people.

19 In the courts of the Lord's house,
    **in the midst of you, O Jerusalem.
    Hallelujah!**

PSALM 118:14-29

14 The Lord is my strength and song,
    and he has become my salvation.

15 There is a sound of exultation and victory
    in the tents of the righteous.

16   'The right hand of the Lord has triumphed!
     the right hand of the Lord is exalted!
     the right hand of the Lord has triumphed!'

17   I shall not die, but live;
     and declare the works of the Lord.

18   The Lord has punished me sorely,
     but he did not hand me over to death.

        *   *   *

19   Open for me the gates of righteousness;
     I will enter them;
     I will offer thanks to the Lord.

20   'This is the gate of the Lord;
     the one who is righteous may enter.'

21   I will give thanks to you, for you answered me
     and have become my salvation.

22   The same stone which the builders rejected
     has become the chief cornerstone.

23   This is the Lord's doing,
     and it is marvellous in our eyes.

24   On this day the Lord has acted;
     we will rejoice and be glad in it.

        *   *   *

25   Hosanna, Lord, hosanna!
     Lord, send us now success.

26   Blessed is he who comes in the name of the Lord;
     we bless you from the house of the Lord.

27   God is the Lord; he has shined upon us;
     form a procession with branches
     up to the horns of the altar.

28 'You are my God, and I will thank you;
   you are my God, and I will exalt you.'

29 Give thanks to the Lord, for he is good;
   his mercy endures for ever.

PSALM 119:1-8

1 Happy are they whose way is blameless,
   who walk in the law of the Lord!

2 Happy are they who observe his decrees
   and seek him with all their hearts!

3 Who never do any wrong,
   but always walk in his ways.

4 You laid down your commandments,
   that we should fully keep them.

5 Oh, that my ways were made so direct
   that I might keep your statutes!

6 Then I should not be put to shame,
   when I regard all your commandments.

7 I will thank you with a sincere heart,
   when I have learned your righteous judgments.

8 I will keep your statutes;
   do not utterly forsake me.

PSALM 119:33-48

33 Teach me, O Lord, the way of your statutes,
   and I shall keep it to the end.

34　Give me understanding, and I shall keep your law;
　　I shall keep it with all my heart.

35　Make me go in the path of your commandments,
　　for that is my desire.

36　Incline my heart to your decrees
　　and not to unjust gain.

37　Turn my eyes from watching what is worthless;
　　give me life in your ways.

38　Fulfil your promise to your servant,
　　which you make to those who fear you.

39　Turn away the reproach which I dread,
　　because your judgments are good.

40　Behold, I long for your commandments;
　　in your righteousness preserve my life.

    *   *   *

41　Let your loving-kindness come to me, O Lord,
　　and your salvation, according to your promise.

42　Then shall I have a word for those who taunt me,
　　because I trust in your words.

43　Do not take the word of truth out of my mouth,
　　for my hope is in your judgments.

44　I shall continue to keep your law;
　　I shall keep it for ever and ever.

45　I will walk at liberty,
　　because I study your commandments.

46　I will tell of your decrees before kings
　　and will not be ashamed.

47 I delight in your commandments,
   which I have always loved.

48 I will lift up my hands to your commandments,
   and I will meditate on your statutes.

PSALM 119:129-136

129 Your decrees are wonderful;
    therefore I obey them with all my heart.

130 When your word goes forth it gives light;
    it gives understanding to the simple.

131 I open my mouth and pant;
    I long for your commandments.

132 Turn to me in mercy,
    as you always do to those who love your name.

133 Steady my footsteps in your word;
    let no iniquity have dominion over me.

134 Rescue me from those who oppress me,
    and I will keep your commandments.

135 Let your countenance shine upon your servant
    and teach me your statutes.

136 My eyes shed streams of tears,
    because people do not keep your law.

PSALM 119:137-144

137 You are righteous, O Lord,
    and upright are your judgments.

138   You have issued your decrees
     with justice and in perfect faithfulness.

139   My indignation has consumed me,
     because my enemies forget your words.

140   Your word has been tested to the uttermost,
     and your servant holds it dear.

141   I am small and of little account,
     yet I do not forget your commandments.

142   Your justice is an everlasting justice
     and your law is the truth.

143   Trouble and distress have come upon me,
     yet your commandments are my delight.

144   The righteousness of your decrees is everlasting;
     grant me understanding, that I may live.

PSALM 121

1   I lift up my eyes to the hills;
     from where is my help to come?

2   My help comes from the Lord,
     the maker of heaven and earth.

3   He will not let your foot be moved
     and he who watches over you will not fall asleep.

4   Behold, he who keeps watch over Israel
     shall neither slumber nor sleep;

5   The Lord himself watches over you;
     the Lord is your shade at your right hand,

6   So that the sun shall not strike you by day,
     nor the moon by night.

7   The Lord shall preserve you from all evil;
     it is he who shall keep you safe.

8   The Lord shall watch over your going out
    and your coming in,
     from this time forth for evermore.

PSALM 122

1   I was glad when they said to me,
     'Let us go to the house of the Lord'.

2   Now our feet are standing
     within your gates, O Jerusalem.

3   Jerusalem is built as a city
     that is at unity with itself.

4   To which the tribes go up,
    the tribes of the Lord,
     the assembly of Israel,
     to praise the name of the Lord.

5   For there are the thrones of judgment,
     the thrones of the house of David.

6   Pray for the peace of Jerusalem:
     'May they prosper who love you.

7   Peace be within your walls
     and quietness within your towers.

8   For my brethren and companions' sake,
     I pray for your prosperity.

9   Because of the house of the Lord our God,
     I will seek to do you good'.

PSALM 124

1 If the Lord had not been on our side,
   let Israel now say;

2 If the Lord had not been on our side,
   when enemies rose up against us;

3 Then would they have swallowed us up alive
   in their fierce anger toward us;

4 Then would the waters have overwhelmed us
   and the torrent gone over us;

5 Then would the raging waters
   have gone right over us.

6 Blessed be the Lord!
   he has not given us over to be a prey for their teeth.

7 We have escaped like a bird from the snare of the fowler;
   the snare is broken, and we have escaped.

8 Our help is in the name of the Lord,
   the maker of heaven and earth.

PSALM 125

1 Those who trust in the Lord are like Mount Zion,
   which cannot be moved, but stands fast for ever.

2 The hills stand about Jerusalem;
   **so does the Lord stand round about his people,
   from this time forth for evermore.**

3 The sceptre of the wicked
   shall not hold sway over the land allotted to the just,
   so that the just shall not put their hands to evil.

4 Show your goodness, O Lord, to those who are good
  and to those who are true of heart.

5 As for those who turn aside to crooked ways,
  the Lord will lead them away with the evildoers;
  but peace be upon Israel.

PSALM 126

1 When the Lord restored the fortunes of Zion,
  then were we like those who dream.

2 Then was our mouth filled with laughter,
  and our tongue with shouts of joy.

  Then they said among the nations,
  'The Lord has done great things for them'.

3 The Lord has done great things for us,
  and we are glad indeed.

4 Restore our fortunes, O Lord,
  like the watercourses of the Negev.

5 Those who sowed with tears
  will reap with songs of joy.

6 Those who go out weeping, carrying the seed,
  will come again with joy, shouldering their sheaves.

PSALM 127

1 Unless the Lord builds the house,
  their labour is in vain who build it.

Unless the Lord watches over the city,
  in vain the watchman keeps his vigil.

2 It is in vain that you rise so early and go to bed so late;
    vain, too, to eat the bread of toil,
    for he gives to his beloved sleep.

3 Children are a heritage from the Lord,
    and the fruit of the womb is a gift.

4 Like arrows in the hand of a warrior
    are the children of one's youth.

5 Happy is the man who has his quiver full of them!
    he shall not be put to shame
    when he contends with his enemies in the gate.

PSALM 128

1 Happy are they who fear the Lord,
    and who follow in his ways!

2 You shall eat the fruit of your labour;
    happiness and prosperity shall be yours.

3 Your wife shall be like a fruitful vine within your house,
    your children like olive shoots round about your table.

4 The one who fears the Lord
    shall thus indeed be blessed.

5 The Lord bless you from Zion,
    and may you see the prosperity of Jerusalem
    all the days of your life.

6 May you live to see your children's children;
    may peace be upon Israel.

PSALM 130

1 Out of the depths have I called you, O Lord;
2 Lord, hear my voice;
   let your ears consider well
   the voice of my supplication.

3 If you, Lord, were to note what is done amiss,
   O Lord, who could stand?

4 For there is forgiveness with you;
   therefore you shall be feared.

5 I wait for the Lord; my soul waits for him;
   in his word is my hope.

6 My soul waits for the Lord,
   more than the watchmen for the morning,
   more than the watchmen for the morning.

7 O Israel, wait for the Lord,
   for with the Lord there is mercy;

8 With him there is plenteous redemption,
   and he shall redeem Israel from all their sins.

PSALM 132: 11-18

11 The Lord has sworn an oath to David;
    in truth, he will not break it:

    'A son, the fruit of your body
    will I set upon your throne.

12 If your children keep my covenant
    and my testimonies that I shall teach them,
    their children will sit upon your throne for evermore'.

13 For the Lord has chosen Zion,
    he has desired her for his habitation:

14 'This shall be my resting-place for ever;
    here will I dwell, for I delight in her.

15 I will surely bless her provisions,
    and satisfy her poor with bread.

16 I will clothe her priests with salvation,
    and her faithful people will rejoice and sing.

17 There will I make the horn of David flourish;
    I have prepared a lamp for my anointed.

18 As for his enemies, I will clothe them with shame;
    but as for him, his crown will shine'.

PSALM 133

1   Oh, how good and pleasant it is,
    when brethren live together in unity!

2   It is like fine oil upon the head
    that runs down upon the beard,

    Upon the beard of Aaron,
    and runs down upon the collar of his robe.

3   It is like the dew of Hermon
    that falls upon the hills of Zion.

    For there the Lord has ordained the blessing:
    life for evermore.

PSALM 135: 1-14

1 Hallelujah!
Praise the name of the Lord;
give praise, you servants of the Lord,

2 You who stand in the house of the Lord,
in the courts of the house of our God.

3 Praise the Lord, for the Lord is good;
sing praises to his name, for it is lovely.

4 For the Lord has chosen Jacob for himself
and Israel for his own possession.

5 For I know that the Lord is great,
and that our Lord is above all gods.

6 The Lord does whatever pleases him,
in heaven and on earth,
in the seas and all the deeps.

7 He brings up rain clouds from the ends of the earth;
he sends out lightning with the rain,
and brings the winds out of his storehouse.

8 It was he who struck down the firstborn of Egypt,
the firstborn both of man and beast.

9 He sent signs and wonders into the midst of you, O Egypt,
against Pharaoh and all his servants.

10 He overthrew many nations
and put mighty kings to death:

11 Sihon, king of the Amorites,
and Og, the king of Bashan,
and all the kingdoms of Canaan.

12 He gave their land to be an inheritance,
an inheritance for Israel his people.

13 O Lord, your name is everlasting;
 your renown, O Lord, endures from age to age.

14 For the Lord gives his people justice
 and shows compassion to his servants.

PSALM 137:1-6

1 By the waters of Babylon we sat down and wept,
 when we remembered you, O Zion.

2 As for our harps, we hung them up
 on the trees in the midst of that land.

3 For those who led us away captive asked us for a song,
 and our oppressors called for mirth:
 'Sing us one of the songs of Zion'.

4 How shall we sing the Lord's song
 upon an alien soil?

5 If I forget you, O Jerusalem,
 let my right hand forget its skill.

6 Let my tongue cleave to the roof of my mouth
 if I do not remember you,
 if I do not set Jerusalem above my highest joy.

PSALM 138

1 I will give thanks to you, O Lord, with my whole heart;
 before the gods I will sing your praise.

2 I will bow down toward your holy temple
 and praise your name,
 because of your love and faithfulness;

For you have glorified your name
  and your word above all things.

3 When I called, you answered me;
  you increased my strength within me.

4 All the kings of the earth will praise you, O Lord,
  when they have heard the words of your mouth.

5 They will sing of the ways of the Lord,
  that great is the glory of the Lord.

6 Though the Lord be high, he cares for the lowly;
  he perceives the haughty from afar.

7 Though I walk in the midst of trouble, you keep me safe;
  you stretch forth your hand
  against the fury of my enemies;
  your right hand shall save me.

8 The Lord will make good his purpose for me;
  O Lord, your love endures for ever;
  do not abandon the works of your hands.

PSALM 139: 1-18

1 Lord, you have searched me out and known me;
2   **you know my sitting down and my rising up;**
  you discern my thoughts from afar.

3 You trace my journeys and my resting-places
  and are acquainted with all my ways.

4 Indeed, there is not a word on my lips,
  but you, O Lord, know it altogether.

5   You press upon me behind and before
    and lay your hand upon me.

6   Such knowledge is too wonderful for me;
    it is so high that I cannot attain to it.

7   Where can I go then from your Spirit?
    where can I flee from your presence?

8   If I climb up to heaven, you are there;
    if I make the grave my bed, you are there also.

9   If I take the wings of the morning
    and dwell in the uttermost parts of the sea,

10 Even there your hand will lead me
    and your right hand hold me fast.

11 If I say, 'Surely the darkness will cover me,
    and the light around me turn to night',

12 Darkness is not dark to you;
    the night is as bright as the day;
    darkness and light to you are both alike.

            *   *   *

13 For you created my inmost parts;
    you knit me together in my mother's womb.

14 I will thank you because I am marvellously made;
    your works are wonderful, and I know it well.

15 My body was not hidden from you,
    while I was being made in secret
    and woven in the depths of the earth.

16 Your eyes beheld my limbs, yet unfinished in the womb;
    all of them were written in your book;
    they were fashioned day by day,
    when as yet there was none of them.

17   How deep I find your thoughts, O God!
      how great is the sum of them!

18   If I were to count them,
      they would be more in number than the sand;
        to count them all,
        my life span would need to be like yours.

PSALM 143:1-10

1   Lord, hear my prayer,
      and in your faithfulness heed my supplications;
        answer me in your righteousness.

2   Enter not into judgment with your servant,
      for in your sight shall no one living be justified.

3   For my enemy has sought my life;
      he has crushed me to the ground;
      he has made me live in dark places
      like those who are long dead.

4   My spirit faints within me;
      my heart within me is desolate..

5   I remember the time past;
      I muse upon all your deeds;
      I consider the works of your hands.

6   I spread out my hands to you;
      my soul gasps to you like a thirsty land.

7   O Lord, make haste to answer me; my spirit fails me;
      do not hide your face from me
      or I shall be like those who go down to the Pit.

8   Let me hear of your loving-kindness in the morning,
    for I put my trust in you;
      show me the road that I must walk,
      for I lift up my soul to you.

9   Deliver me from my enemies, O Lord,
      for I flee to you for refuge.

10 Teach me to do what pleases you, for you are my God;
      let your good Spirit lead me on level ground.

PSALM 145:8-21

8   The Lord is gracious and full of compassion,
      slow to anger and of great kindness.

9   The Lord is loving to everyone
      and his compassion is over all his works.

10 All your works praise you, O Lord,
      and your faithful servants bless you.

11 They make known the glory of your kingdom
      and speak of your power.

12 That the peoples may know of your power
      and the glorious splendour of your kingdom.

13a Your kingdom is an everlasting kingdom;
      your dominion endures throughout all ages.

              *   *   *

13b The Lord is faithful in all his words
      and merciful in all his deeds.

14 The Lord upholds all those who fall;
      he lifts up those who are bowed down.

15 The eyes of all wait upon you, O Lord,
      and you give them their food in due season.

16 You open wide your hand
      and satisfy the needs of every living creature.

17 The Lord is righteous in all his ways
      and loving in all his works.

18 The Lord is near to those who call upon him,
      to all who call upon him faithfully.

19 He fulfils the desire of those who fear him,
      he hears their cry and helps them.

20 The Lord preserves all those who love him,
      but he destroys all the wicked.

21 My mouth shall speak the praise of the Lord;
      let all flesh bless his holy name for ever and ever.

PSALM 146

1 Hallelujah!
    Praise the Lord, O my soul!
2 **I will praise the Lord as long as I live;**
    I will sing praises to my God while I have my being.

3 Put not your trust in rulers, nor in any child of earth,
    for there is no help in them.

4 When they breathe their last, they return to earth,
    and in that day their thoughts perish.

5 Happy are they who have the God of Jacob for their help!
    whose hope is in the Lord their God;

6   Who made heaven and earth, the seas,
    and all that is in them;
        who keeps his promise for ever;

7   Who gives justice to those who are oppressed,
        and food to those who hunger.

    The Lord sets the prisoners free;
8   the Lord opens the eyes of the blind;
        the Lord lifts up those who are bowed down;

    The Lord loves the righteous;
9   the Lord cares for the stranger;
        he sustains the orphan and widow,
        but frustrates the way of the wicked.

10 The Lord shall reign for ever,
        your God, O Zion, throughout all generations.
        Hallelujah!

    PSALM 147

1   Hallelujah!
    How good it is to sing praises to our God!
        how pleasant it is to honour him with praise!

2   The Lord rebuilds Jerusalem;
        he gathers the exiles of Israel.

3   He heals the brokenhearted
        and binds up their wounds.

4   He counts the number of the stars
        and calls them all by their names.

5   Great is our Lord and mighty in power;
        there is no limit to his wisdom.

6 The Lord lifts up the lowly,
    but casts the wicked to the ground.

7 Sing to the Lord with thanksgiving;
    make music to our God upon the harp.

8 He covers the heavens with clouds
    and prepares rain for the earth;

9 He provides food for flocks and herds
    and for the young ravens when they cry.

10 He is not impressed by the might of a horse,
    he has no pleasure in the strength of a man;

11 But the Lord has pleasure in those who fear him,
    in those who await his gracious favour.

          *   *   *

12 Worship the Lord, O Jerusalem;
    praise your God, O Zion;

13 For he has strengthened the bars of your gates;
    he has blessed your children within you.

14 He has established peace on your borders;
    he satisfies you with the finest wheat.

15 He sends out his command to the earth,
    and his word runs very swiftly.

16 He gives snow like wool;
    he scatters hoarfrost like ashes.

17 He scatters his hail like bread crumbs;
    who can stand against his cold?

18 He sends forth his word and melts them;
    he blows with his wind, and the waters flow.

19 He declares his word to Jacob,
   his statutes and his judgments to Israel.

20 He has not done so to any other nation;
   to them he has not revealed his judgments.
   Hallelujah!

PSALM 149

1 Hallelujah!
  Sing to the Lord a new song:
  sing his praise in the congregation of the faithful.

2 Let Israel rejoice in their maker;
  let the children of Zion be joyful in their king.

3 Let them praise his name in the dance;
  let them sing praise to him with timbrel and harp.

4 For the Lord takes pleasure in his people
  and adorns the poor with victory.

5 Let the faithful rejoice in triumph;
  let them be joyful on their beds.

6 Let the praises of God be in their throat
  and a two-edged sword in their hand;

7 To wreak vengeance on the nations
  and punishment on the peoples;

8 To bind their kings in chains
  and their nobles with links of iron;

9 To inflict on them the judgment decreed;
  this is glory for all his faithful people.
  Hallelujah!

PSALM 150

1 Hallelujah!
Praise God in his holy temple;
  praise him in the firmament of his power.

2 Praise him for his mighty acts;
  praise him for his excellent greatness.

3 Praise him with the blast of the ram's-horn;
  praise him with lyre and harp.

4 Praise him with timbrel and dance;
  praise him with strings and pipe.

5 Praise him with resounding cymbals;
  praise him with loud-clanging cymbals.

6 Let everything that has breath
  praise the Lord.
  Hallelujah!

Acknowledgments

Acknowledgments

Over the last few years, ecumenically and internationally, English-speaking churches have witnessed a convergence in both the liturgical shape of orders of service and in translations of texts which churches have in common.

During the years of preparation of *Uniting in Worship*, The Assembly Commission on Liturgy has enjoyed a growing relationship with many other worship commissions and committees in the English-speaking world. These groups include the following:

The Australian Consultation on Liturgy (ACOL)
The Liturgical Commission of The Anglican Church of Australia
The worship committees of other member churches of The Australian Consultation on Liturgy
The English Language Liturgical Consultation (ELLC)
The Faith and Order Committee of The Methodist Church, U.K.
The General Synod Liturgical Commission of The Church of England, U.K.
The Church of Scotland Panel on Worship, U.K.
The Committee for Doctrine and Worship of The United Reformed Church, U.K.
The Doctrine and Worship Committee of The Anglican Church of Canada
The Worship Office, Division of Mission in Canada, The United Church of Canada
The Board of Congregational Life, The Presbyterian Church in Canada
The Standing Liturgical Commission of The Episcopal Church, U.S.A.
The Office of Worship, The Presbyterian Church (U.S.A.)
The International Commission on English in the Liturgy – A Joint Commission of Catholic Bishops' Conferences
The Section on Worship, The General Board of Discipleship, The United Methodist Church, U.S.A.
The Office for Church Life and Leadership, The United Church of Christ, U.S.A.
The Faith and Order Committee of The Methodist Church of New Zealand
The Worship Committee of The Presbyterian Church of New Zealand

These groups have generously shared published resources, journals and newsletters, and exchanged correspondence with us. Our indebtedness to some of these groups for the amount of material taken from their publications is very great. But all the groups listed above have in some way assisted our work. While much of the content of *Uniting in Worship*, particularly the orders of service, is the original work of the Commission, members of the above groups will recognise a phrase here or a sentence there which has been inspired by their own work.

Scripture quotations are from the *Revised Standard Version of the Bible*, copyrighted 1946, 1952, © 1971, 1973 by the Division of Christian Education of the National Council of the Churches of Christ in the U.S.A., and used by permission. A number of very small changes to the R.S.V. text have been made for the sake of inclusive language.

The English translations of *The Lord's Prayer, Apostles' Creed, Nicene Creed* (adapted), *'Lord, have mercy', 'Glory to God in the highest', 'Lift up your hearts', 'Holy, holy, holy Lord', 'Lamb of God', 'Glory to the Father', 'We praise you, O God', Song of Zechariah, Song of Mary* and *Song of Simeon* were originally prepared by the International Consultation on English Texts (ICET) and revised in 1987 by the English Language Liturgical Consultation (ELLC).

The Selections from The Psalter and other excerpts from the psalms used elsewhere are taken from *The Psalter* of *The Book of Common Prayer*, 1979, of The Episcopal Church, U.S.A. Other resources from *The Book of Common Prayer* include some of the canticles and litanies, some prayers in Resources for the Liturgical Year and Resources for Leading Worship, and prayers in several orders of service. Used with approval.

Four of the litanies are from *The Worshipbook Services*. Copyright © 1970, The Westminster Press, Philadelphia, PA, U.S.A. Adapted and used by permission.

Two great prayers of thanksgiving and one other prayer in The Service of the Lord's Day and some prayers in Resources for Leading Worship are from *The Service for the Lord's Day - (Supplemental Liturgical Resource 1)*. Prepared by The Office of Worship, The Presbyterian Church (U.S.A.) Copyright © 1984, The Westminster Press, Philadelphia, PA, U.S.A. Used by permission.

The two prayers of thanksgiving in both services of baptism have been inspired by work published in *Holy Baptism and Services for The Renewal of Baptism - (Supplemental Liturgical Resource 2)*. Copyright © 1985, The Westminster Press, Philadelphia, PA, U.S.A.

Two prayers in The Marriage Service are from *Christian Marriage - (Supplemental Liturgical Resource 3)*. Copyright © 1986, The Westminster Press, Philadelphia, PA, U.S.A. Used by permission.

Some of the prayers in A Treasury of Prayers are from *The Book of Common Prayer*, 1662. The Commission gratefully acknowledges that this book is the heritage of The Church of England and affirms that, other than the Bible itself, no other book has provided so great an enrichment both of English literature and also of christian devotion in the Reformed tradition.

The form of The Covenant Service is based on that in *The Methodist Service Book*, 1975. One Great Prayer of Thanksgiving in The Service of the Lord's Day, one prayer in The Marriage Service, some prayers in The Funeral Service and three thanksgivings and other prayers in Resources for Leading Worship are also from *The Methodist Service Book*. Used by permission of The Methodist Faith and Order Committee and The Methodist Publishing House, London.

One great Prayer of Thanksgiving and other prayers in The Service of the Lord's Day are from the text of Second Order of The Holy Communion of *An Australian Prayer Book*, 1978, copyright, The Anglican Church of Australia Trust Corporation. Some prayers in The Marriage Service, The Funeral Service, Resources for Leading Worship and A Treasury of Prayers are also from this book. Some of the collects in Resources for the Liturgical Year are from *An Australian Prayer Book* or *Alternative Collects*, both published by the Anglican Information Office. Reproduced with permission.

The Ordination Prayer in Ordination of a Minister of the Word is based on *An Ordinal – The United Methodist Church*. Copyright © 1979 by The Board of Discipleship of The United Methodist Church. Used by permission.

Some of the collects in Resources for the Liturgical Year and some of the prayers in Resources for Leading Worship have been written by The Revd Dr Peter Gardner, a minister of The Presbyterian Church of New Zealand and a valued consultant to the Commission. Used with permission.

The Commission gratefully acknowledges the work of Liturgy Training Publications, Chicago, Illinois, in publishing a 3-year cycle of opening prayers, based on the *Roman Lectionary*. This initiative in the U.S.A. has encouraged the Commission to prepare a similar 3-year cycle of collects, based on the readings in *Common Lectionary*. Some of the collects included in Resources for the Liturgical Year are the opening prayers prepared by The Revd Peter Scagnelli and published by Liturgy Training Publications; other collects prepared by the Commission have been inspired by his work.

The Scripture lections set out in Resources for the Liturgical Year for Sundays and other principal days are those of *Common Lectionary*, prepared by the Consultation on Common Texts of North America.

Some of the collects in Resources for the Liturgical Year are reprinted from *Lutheran Book of Worship*, copyright © 1978, by permission of Augsburg Publishing House, Minneapolis.

Two of the canticles are adapted from *Praise God in Song*, copyright © 1979 by G.I.A. Publications, Inc., Chicago, Illinois. All rights reserved.

Three prayers in Resources for Leading Worship are from *Contemporary Prayers for Public Worship*, edited by Caryl Micklem, © 1967 SCM Press Ltd. Used by permission.

'A Litany for Advent' is from *Praise in All Our Days: Common Prayer at Taizé*, Mowbrays, Oxford, 1975. Used by permission.

The prayer 'Bearers of Reconciliation' by Brother Roger of Taize is from *Praying Together in Word and Song*, Mowbrays, Oxford, 1985. Used by permission.

Every effort has been made to trace owners of copyright and to obtain permission to include material in *Uniting in Worship*. If, through inadvertence, appropriate acknowledgment has not been made, the Commission and its publisher would be pleased to be notified and will rectify such omissions in future printings.

Grant Dunning
Secretary
Assembly Commission on Liturgy
March, 1988